BACK CAST

JEFF METCALF
BACK CAST

FLY-FISHING
AND OTHER SUCH MATTERS

THE UNIVERSITY OF UTAH PRESS
Salt Lake City

The Defiance House Man colophon is a registered trademark
of The University of Utah Press. It is based on a four-foot-tall
Ancient Puebloan pictograph (late PIII) near Glen Canyon, Utah.

LIBRARY OF CONGRESS CATALOGING-IN-PUBLICATION DATA
Names: Metcalf, Jeff, author.
Title: Back cast : fly-fishing and other such matters / Jeff Metcalf.
Description: Salt Lake City : The University of Utah Press, [2018] |
    Identifiers: LCCN 2017049900 (print) | LCCN 2017051150 (ebook) | ISBN
    9781607816133 () | ISBN 9781607816126 (pbk.)
Subjects: LCSH: Fly fishing—Utah—Anecdotes. | Fly
    fishing—Idaho—Anecdotes. | Cancer—Patients—Biography. | Fly
    fishing—Social aspects.
Classification: LCC SH464.W4 (ebook) | LCC SH464.W4 M48 2018 (print)
| DDC
    799.12/409796—dc23
LC record available at https://lccn.loc.gov/2017049900

Epigraph quotation from Sparse Grey Hackle, *Fishless Days, Angling Nights:
Classic Stories, Reminiscences, and Lore.* New York: Crown, 1972.

The Theodore Roethke poem quoted in the chapter "Death Song" is "Praise
to the End!", from *The Collected Poems of Theodore Roethke.* New York:
Anchor Books, 1975.

Printed and bound in the United States of America.

A portion of the proceeds of the sales of this book will go to the Henry's
Fork Foundation.

for
Alana, Bailey, John, Jack, and Finn,
and for my sibling
Sue

"If fishing interferes with your business, give up your business," any angler will tell you, citing instances of men who lost health and even life through failure to take a little recreation, and reminding you that 'the trout do not rise in the Green Wood Cemetery,' so you had better do your fishing while you are still able. But you will search far to find a fisherman to admit that a taste for fishing, like a taste for liquor, must be governed lest it come to possess its possessor; that an excess of fishing can cause as many tragedies of lost purpose, earning power, and position as an excess of liquor."

—SPARSE GREY HACKLE, *Fishless Days, Angling Nights*

CONTENTS

BONE DEEP

Last fall a group of seventeen men, all strangers to each other, met for the first time to fly-fish together at one of Utah's most pristine series of private trout ponds, belonging to Falcon's Ledge Lodge in Altamont, Utah. The men came from various parts of the state and were the guests of a program called Reel Recovery, which brings men together for three days of fly-fishing and conversation about their lives, specifically how they are dealing with their cancer. If there is a catch—no pun intended—it is based on the simple idea that men, unlike women, need to learn how to talk about their own health issues. And men need to talk with each other. So bring them together where there are beautiful trout, teach the art of fly-fishing, and invite them to talk.

I'd read about the program in *Trout Unlimited*, and I was intrigued by the idea. Each man in the program would work with a volunteer guide, a buddy, whose primary job would be to teach the basics of fly-fishing. For part of three days, the Reel Recovery participants would have their own private trout guide. This was an idea I found most appealing. For over forty years I had fished the great trout waters of the West and thought that giving back in such a fashion was meaningful and important. Earlier in the year I had contacted Reel Recovery headquarters and offered my services as a guide. To my pleasant surprise, I was given the dates, contact points, and directions to Falcon Ledge. On the given day, I was the first to arrive, equipped with extra waders, fishing vests, fly rods, reels, boxes of flies, and a variety of different-sized boots tucked into my kit.

I introduced myself at the front desk and waited for my instructions. It seemed logical that once the men arrived there would be
some sort of general orientation and then perhaps the guides would
be introduced to their partners. With that in the back of my mind,
I was surprised when one of the facilitators welcomed me to the
lodge and offered to show me to my room.

"I thought the guides either camped out or drove themselves
to the retreat on a daily basis."

"That's right."

"Then I really don't need a room. I'm planning on camping out."

"But the participants in Reel Recovery have a room in the lodge."

"I volunteered to guide," I replied politely.

"Let's check this out," he said, walking back to the check-in desk.
After a few moments he looked up from his ledger. "We've got you
down as a participant."

"I think there's a mistake."

"It says in the application that you have prostate cancer."

"I do. But actually, I signed up to guide."

"You filled out the wrong form. We've got you down as a
participant."

"But I don't think I need it. I'd rather—"

"Let me show you to your room and you can decide whether
you want to stay or not. We'd love to have you join us. And honestly, if you're not a participant it sort of messes up the pairings."

Once I saw the view from the room it was all over. Beneath
me, gently spread out in folds against the landscape, lay several still
ponds stocked with trout. A knuckle of a rise bubbled from a brown
trout slurping a fly from an evening hatch.

"This is fabulous," I said. "I'd be happy to be a participant."

At the time, I had no idea that I was in need of such a retreat.
This epiphany would be revealed to me in the coming three days.
But at that moment, the world seemed perfect. In the evening, we
all met in a circle on the main floor of the lodge. In turn we introduced ourselves to the group and answered a few questions about

our lives. The facilitators for the evening guided us along. The questions: simple enough. Name. Profession. Our favorite car growing up. Safe manly stuff. Finally, just before we broke for dinner, a different direction, one I sensed would continue to be the focus of the remaining two days. *What type of cancer do you have and how has it made you feel?*

These responses were much more guarded and cautious. We knew if we spoke truthfully and openly we would enter into the realm of self-revelation. This is not a place where men are comfortable being. It is too dangerous, too vulnerable. We have trained well to guard ourselves.

We were truly a mixed bag of men. There is little doubt we would not have collected together under any other circumstance. Among our ranks were the president of a bank, a former cab driver, a retired railroad engineer, a lifer in the United States Army, a filmmaker, a professor of English, a plumber, a world arm-wrestling champion, a brick mason, a Marine who did two active tours of duty in Vietnam, and a police officer. Two of the participants— Tuck, a retired railroad engineer, and Ed, his cousin and a three-time world arm-wrestling champion—were two of the first men I met at the retreat. In the circle on that first evening, they sat to my left. Tuck, a handsome, rugged man, and Ed, who was at the time fighting three different cancers, were not interested in this touchy-feely public display of emotions. But the facilitators wouldn't allow that as a satisfactory response. It became clear that silence, in carrying the weight of our cancers, had not served us well.

One of the original founders of the Reel Recovery program, who happened to be a facilitator, was pointed in his comments to the group. "I invite you during these three days to share your truth about cancer. The more you share this truth with each other, the more freedom you have."

After a few moments of uncomfortable silence, he continued: "We share a legacy as men. We have gathered in circles for thousands of years to prepare for battles, to discuss strategy and purpose.

Men have gathered after battles to discuss what worked, what didn't, and the men they lost. They have blessed each other, consoled each other, and rejoiced together in these circles."

The room became silent. At that moment, I realized I was in for more than I'd bargained for, or at least I thought so, and this surprised me. I was in for something I needed deeply and that was the theme: *courageous conversation of men with cancer.* We studied each other to see who would pick up the gauntlet.

Finally Ed, a tree trunk of a man even with his cancer, broke the silence and began to talk about his illness and how it had changed his life. He spoke of the pain he believed he had caused his family by having cancer. His voice was almost inaudible as he spoke of having to deal with something he couldn't conquer with his bare hands. "When I look at myself in the mirror and see all the scars on my body, I feel like Frankenstein. I don't know how my wife can touch me."

As Ed spoke, I watched his cousin Tuck, the most vociferous among us, who had talked about not having any interest in the "circle jerk" of emotional intimacy. Tuck had his head down. His arms were resting on his knees and it was clear he was having a difficult time holding things together. In truth, he was not the only one in the group barely holding on. And then Ed put us all over the top when he spoke of his two boys, Hunter and Fisher.

"I don't feel like I've been much of a father to my boys. They are having a difficult time with this and they're angry and I can't do anything about this. I feel worthless. I don't feel like a husband or a father and sometimes," he paused, wiping tears from his eyes, "I wonder if they wouldn't be better off without me."

Tuck began to cry. He reached over and as gracefully and gently as I have ever seen one human comfort another, he took his cousin's hand and squeezed it softly. From that moment on, we were all changed. Ed's utterly self-revealing honesty, his laying out of his darkest and most intimate secrets in front of a group of strangers, was perhaps one of the bravest and most generous displays I have ever witnessed. This simple act of charity disarmed us and granted us permission to tell our own stories. And we did. Each man in turn offered up what was most private and unspoken. I found myself talking about the most carefully guarded secrets in my dealings with cancer. Never could I have imagined.

The fly-fishing was brilliant. During the three-day retreat, all seventeen men caught fish. And in those sweet moments—the length of time between the cast and the rise of a plump trout to the fly— we were all free of our cancer.

I entered into the weekend with the belief that I would be a *buddy* to men who had cancer and had never fly-fished before. Had that been the case, I would have left the retreat with a feeling that I had given something of myself to men who were in need. Instead, it was I who was the recipient of their generosity and brotherhood; it was I who was in great need.

Six of the men I fished with that fall have passed away since I began writing this collection of essays. Three or four others have had their cancers return, including myself. Whenever I am on a river, I carry these men with me. And when I catch a plump trout, I name it for one of my brothers and release it back into the wild, where it disappears into the sacred and holy.

THE REEL

In a way it held more magic than Christmas Eve. I had butterflies and couldn't get to sleep. No matter what position I curled into nor how hard I tried to invoke the sandman to help out, I inevitably found myself drawn to the magic of the four gifts given to me by my grandfather, Pops.

The gifts? They were simple enough. A wax-paper bag with three shiny fishing hooks inside. A brand-new spool of fishing line with a bobber. An old bamboo fishing pole. As for the fourth gift, it was the most special of all: a well-oiled, slightly bent, second-hand fishing reel given to my grandfather by one of his card-playing buddies. To me, it was a gift of immeasurable value and status. It was a treasure that granted me unchallenged respect from my circle of boyhood friends, and I was careful to guard that position.

IT TOOK FOREVER for spring to arrive. By the time it did, I had been ready for nearly four months. So when my grandfather picked me up, as promised, I was ready. I had followed his directions carefully. With some reluctance our next-door neighbor, Mrs. Dinunzio, had allowed me to dig for worms in her small garden plot. I unearthed six worms and placed them into a coffee can covered with dirt. It was not without a price, however, since I felt compelled to offer her the first catch of the day.

"Where ya gonna catch fish in New York?" she chuckled.

"I don't know. Wherever Pops says," I answered. "He knows a secret place."

"We'll have a big feast when you get back," she cackled, and then she pinched me on the cheek—which I couldn't stand—and wished me luck. For the worms and a day of fishing with my grandfather, I could stand anything.

My grandfather took me to Silver Lake Park on Staten Island. It was only a few blocks from the tenement building we grew up in, but the park was paradise. For a boy of five, it was the home of Robin Hood, Zorro, Roy Rogers, and soon to be remembered as the place where Moby Dick was caught.

We walked hand in hand to the lake and my grandfather talked the entire way. He told me some of his secrets about fishing, which I am afraid were wasted on me. On a park bench he demonstrated how to hook up the reel and the pole. After this, he took the reel off the pole and had me put it back on. I did it without a single mistake. He complimented me and told me I would make a fine fisherman, and I glowed in the praise. I held the spool of line while my grandfather reeled it through the eyes of the pole. Finally, he taught me how to tie the hook on using one of the most basic knots of life and showed me how to attach the worm to the hook properly.

With a few lessons on how to cast, he let me go. I attacked the water. My first cast never made it into the lake and landed with a thump just in front of my feet. My second cast was not much better. On the fifth or sixth try, my line sailed into the air and landed, battered worm and all, in Silver Lake. I was ecstatic and promptly forgot what to do next. Again my grandfather guided me, and soon I was able to cast and reel with little difficulty.

The morning continued much in the same fashion; the teacher and the pupil, the grandfather and the grandson. After the last of the worms vanished into the lake, my grandfather bought us hot dogs and soft drinks from a park vendor and we had lunch. He listened carefully as I told him about the fish I thought had struck my bait. Never once did he doubt or challenge me and never once did he tell me that there were no fish in Silver Lake. I found that out many years later, and it made no difference at all.

I TAUGHT MY son and daughter how to fish. It was in a pond to the side of a country club. We used the same old bamboo pole and slightly bent reel. When they grew up, I taught them how to fly-fish, and we fished the great waters of the Rocky Mountains. They became beautiful casters and followed the water in their own ways.

I am sixty-seven years old as of this writing and I have just become a grandfather for the second time—to our daughter's second son. Her oldest, Jack, is five years old, and soon I will take him to catch his first trout in the Sawtooth Mountains. Finn, his younger brother, is not old enough, but when he is I will do the same for him.

Both my grandfather and father passed away many years ago. The bamboo pole was broken when I was jousting as Sir Lancelot in front of Queen Guinevere, my sister. But I still have the reel, well oiled, and I hope it offers as much magic to my grandsons as it did to me.

HOOKED

All fly fishermen come to the water first through a spinning rig and
a worm, then a variety of spinning lures and, if they are enlightened,
through the fly rod and delicately tied flies. It is not an easy transformation and it requires, among other things, a degree of patience,
a renunciation of the satisfying plunk of weighted tackle, and the
abandonment of collapsible folding chairs and a beer cooler for the
soft swish of a fly line and the delivery of a small fly that must be
presented perfectly on the water for any trout to remotely consider
striking such a modest representation of an insect. My conversion
was by circumstance and not by choice.

As a young boy I was fortunate to live in the Middle East for
four years, with the Persian Gulf and Half Moon Bay not far from
my home. My father worked for Arabian American Oil Company,
and I began sea fishing off the dock at the ex-pats' yacht club along
with young Arab boys my own age. I would put shrimp on the end
of a hand line and hurl it into the depths of the gulf, landing fish
that I would then gladly turn over to these boys, who took the pan-
sized fish home to their families.

During the summer months I sold Kool-Aid popsicles at the
Dhahran swimming pool until I earned enough money to purchase
a spear gun, a good mask, and flippers so I could begin hunting
beneath the surface for larger prey. By the time I was twelve years
old, I'd killed pickhandle barracuda, a variety of large sea grouper,
silver biddy, and sergeant majors, and once even shot a sand shark,
almost drowning in the process. I was a killing machine, and some

fifty years later I still feel great sorrow that I ate very few of those fish. I have made my penance over the passing of time.

Eventually I began deep-sea fishing with good tackle, heavy-duty reels, and sturdy sea poles, and attached myself to anybody willing to drag me along on a weekend adventure.

When we returned to the United States, the thought of fishing for freshwater trout with a spinning rig on Western rivers held no magic at all. I was a boy of the ocean, brave or stupid enough to climb into shark-infested waters and hunt. How could this compare? When my buddies spoke of landing a big two- or three-pound trout, I remained silent.

Later in life, in a late-night college poker game, I drew four honest aces in seven-card stud and won, from an East Coast boy that I was not particularly fond of, a pair of heavy rubber Red Ball waders, a West Yellowstone fly rod, a Shakespeare fly reel, a brittle fly line permanently coiled with age, and a fishing vest.

Following my graduation from college, I purchased an acre parcel of land in the Uinta Mountains in northeastern Utah and spent my summer months building a cabin that sat above a sweeping vista of the forest, complete with a small meandering stream that ran through the property. In the process of stocking the cabin with cooking utensils, second-hand furniture, and anything in my home that might be of use, I came back across the fly-fishing gear. I hauled it up to the cabin with no intention of ever using it, but thinking it would look *cool* at the cabin alongside my snowshoes and rusty collection of interesting pieces I'd scrounged from dumps and old mining camps. The cabin would be the place I became a famous novelist. It had everything a writer required: solitude, cheap booze just across the state line in Wyoming, a natural wilderness setting, and the provision of uninterrupted time.

I am by nature a restless soul who would rather hike through backcountry than write about it. In a moment of absolute weakness, I made a tremendous mistake, one that I have paid for all of my life. I decided to give fly-fishing a go. The gear was in front of me, and I had plenty of streams and rivers surrounding the cabin. What harm could come of it?

Doc Olsen's fly shop was an old-school, classic western fly shop. Doc sold flies, fly line, tippet material, vests, rods and reels, creels, and anything connected to this silly sport, so I paid him a visit and explained my dilemma. By the time I left his shop, I'd purchased a tin fly box that I'd filled with flies, a new line, some floatant, and a net at the cost of—if I remember correctly—just over thirty dollars. I headed to the water to see what this was all about. Doc had drawn me a map of the Bear River and placed an X on the three spots that he thought might produce fish.

When I pulled my Volkswagen camper into the first spot, there were already three other fly fishermen casting to and landing trout. Watching them cast completely confused me. It wasn't like slinging metal, where one unlocks the line, holds a thumb over the drag, and casts a lure forty yards into the water. It seemed, at first appearance, that these men wasted a great deal of time getting the fly onto water, engaged in a cast that required several metronome-like motions before letting the fly settle down on the river. But, I easily admit now, it was a beautiful thing to watch.

I should have tried on the waders. When I climbed into them and cinched up my suspenders, I realized the error of my ways. The young man whom I'd relieved of his fly-fishing equipment in the poker game was easily six inches taller than me, and the waders came up to my armpits. That turned out to be the least of my problems. A few minutes after climbing into the river, I began to feel water seeping into the waders. They'd been folded and stored in a warm basement and were filled with crack-line leaks on the fold. There wasn't a great deal of water but it was steady. I could handle the leaks because it was a hot Utah day and the water felt cool against my skin.

Casting seriously confounded me. The first attempt landed the fly about a foot from where I was standing. How did those other men get so much line out? Subsequent casts were no better, and since none of the fly fishermen seemed remotely interested in what I was doing I studied their techniques. I soon noticed that to get the fly out some distance required having excess line opposite the casting hand. It made sense because I understood that the line also became the weight to shoot the line onto the water. It was unclear whether these men let the line stretch out behind them or in front of them when they completed the cast. So I flailed away. Soon I was able to get about fifteen feet of line out consistently but it slapped at the water when it landed.

Men get cocky when we feel like we've conquered something new. Although I knew my technique was not yet fluid, I did feel that with a little practice I might be able to master this form. However, on a particularly terrible lift off the water my Royal Coachman fly with a barbed hook came shooting back toward my face. I did not duck, and it embedded itself painfully and deeply into the fat of my cheek. I checked to see if the other fly fishermen had heard me yelp. Apparently not, so I tried several unsuccessful attempts to dislodge the fly from my face. I couldn't. Instead, I snipped the fly off at the eye and left it. I'd take it out later. Then I tied on an Adams dry fly. This time I would pay attention. I made two casts before I was able to sink this fly deep into my earlobe. Again, unsuccessfully, I attempted to disengage the fly. My lobe was bleeding and beginning to swell. I cut the tippet off and left the fly in my ear. Any reasonably intelligent man, any moderately intelligent man, would have taken these two events as a sign from the gods that this was not a sport in which he should engage and would have climbed out of the water never to return. I was not that man. Instead, I withdrew my fly box and selected another fly, a Parachute Adams, and cinched it tightly to my line.

I should have known what would happen next. The muse had warned me—the omens were already stuck in my face. It was the most horrible thing conceivable. I ginked the Adams and made two rather decent casts. My third cast landed on a bush lining the bank. It hung lightly on a branch and the hook did not appear to be sunk into timber. Ever so delicately I gave the line a twitch, and the fly alighted on the water. I did not have time to appreciate this nuance because instantly something silver slashed to the fly and ripped into it. Here now is a sequence of what I think happened next: I screamed (I'm certain of this); I jerked my fly rod high above my head; I let go of all the line I had in my left hand, creating tremendous slack and losing the tension on the fly; I stumbled on rock as I stepped back in the river, lost my balance, and fell sideways into the water. I took a little water into my waders and my heart was pumping. When I managed to regain my footing the fly line was spaghetti on the river and, more disappointing, there wasn't any tension on my line. The fish was off the fly. I began reeling in the excess line when it suddenly tugged and began moving upstream. The fish was still on the line! My god, I hadn't cocked it all up after all! I managed successfully to land a beautiful little rainbow trout no more than twelve inches long. It was one of the smallest fish I'd ever landed in my life, but I can't begin to explain the sensation I felt at that moment. I had figured out something important. I knew deep down that somehow the water would call me back and the river would remain, forever, in my life.

THREE DOWN

I would like to say that I came to fly-fishing in an ancestral way; that my grandfather had handed down his split-cane rod to my father, who in turn passed it on to me when I had come of proper age. That on any given summer evening we had, all three of us, walked the banks of the Beaverkill River, casting to rising trout, finding ourselves alone at the pocket water of Horse Brook Run, a blanket hatch of black caddis and blue quill in the golden light of an early summer evening.

And later in this dream, on the way to the river, the men would let me run ahead, empty wicker basket slung across my back, bouncing rhythmically against my hips, and they would allow me "first shot" at filling the creel with plump trout for dinner. My grand-father and my father, Jackson, would lazily walk the banks, pulling from their flasks and smoking Camel cigarettes. Sometimes, over my back cast, I could see them watching me. It was a great feeling, as though I had been secretly inducted into their world, a world of smoke and alcohol, rivers and trout. It's the story I would like to tell, but it would be far from the truth.

Instead, the year was 1968, in the small college town of Logan, Utah. It was a crisp winter night, and the temperature held tight at five degrees. There was an illegal card game being held in a cramped room in the High Rise dorm. There was alcohol and cigar smoke and plenty of testosterone. It was strictly illegal for any of this to be taking place but the floor jock, Burr, had weightier problems on his mind.

The North Vietnamese had launched the Tet Offensive, and the North Koreans had just hijacked the USS Pueblo three days earlier.

Burr was a member of the active reserve for the US Navy and was worried he might be called up immediately for duty. He had mentioned this to a bunch of us at the mess hall. It was a critical mistake to offer this information to a group of immature young men.

That Friday, following several hours of drinking beer at the Bistro in downtown Logan, three of us sent Burr a Western Union telegram ordering him to report back to his unit in New Jersey for active duty.

The night of the poker game, Lug Nuts told us Burr had been activated and was already packing his duffle bags. Rumor was that he'd booked a ticket on a Greyhound bus and would be heading for the East Coast to see his girlfriend before shipping out. The joke had gone over the top and somebody had to tell him, probably me since it had been my idea. But the poker game was on.

Several hours into the night, Lump interrupted the usual banter, "Hey, anybody got any Drambuie? We're out."

"No, but I'll bet Burr has some," I offered. Since I'd folded early on the hand, I volunteered to walk down the hall to his room and borrow some.

Outside the door, I could hear the Irish Rovers' rendition of "The Drunken Sailor" playing on his stereo. I knocked on the door. Nothing. On the second knock, he opened the door. His eyes were raw and puffy as though he'd been crying.

"Jesus, Burr, what's going on?"

"Want a drink?"

"Sure." I entered. The ashtray on his night table spilled over with cigarette butts. He poured a healthy Irish whiskey in a jelly jar and handed it to me. He gestured for me to sit down.

"Did you hear what happened to me today?"

"Yes," I answered.

"How fucked up is that?"

"It's fucked."

Before I could say anything, he handed me a stack of albums from Tower of Power, the Chieftains, some Motown bands, and my favorite Irish Rovers collection.

"For you."

"I can't take these," I said, pushing them away.

"Bullshit. You've been a good friend."

"I haven't."

He stared at me, and for a moment I thought he'd figured things out.

"I'm the one who sent that telegram to you."

He didn't believe me. "Fuck you! That's not funny," he said, smiling. "It's really not funny."

"I know, but I did and I'm very sorry."

He stared at me for the longest time. When I stood up, I was prepared for anything he'd dish out. Whatever it was, I deserved it. He took the glass from my hand. I braced myself. It was swift and brutal.

"Leave my room."

"Burr, I don't know how to—"

"I will never talk to you again, Metty. Ever."

And he didn't.

When I finished telling the story to the boys around the poker table, Pin, a thug from Boston, simply said, "Fuck him if he can't take a joke." I was not overly fond of Pin.

"*You* didn't have to tell him," I shot back. "You chicken-shitted out of it. All of us did."

"Because it was your idea, Metty."

I had not been playing poker well that night. I bought cards I had no right to buy, folded too early, made bad bets, bluffed when I shouldn't have. Pin's dismissal of my confession to Burr brought me back though. Over the next hour I gained back most of my losses, enough so that I could hold out against anyone at the table if need be.

On what eventually turned out to be the final hand of the night, I drew an ace and jack down with the Big Casino up on the first three cards. A long-shot straight. I couldn't tell much by looking at the table. Lump showed a queen; Vegas, a jake; and Pin, the king of spades. Pin bet big. I guessed him for a pair. The other players, nothing of note showing, stayed with the first bet.

My next card was an ace up, so I had a pair of bullets. It was my bet so I began with Pin's previous bet. Nobody folded and when it came to Pin, he raised the bet, which in turn was called and raised again. The pot was building. I figured Pin for a pair of kings, which gave me the better hand, but since I didn't see any kings elsewhere on the table, he could possibly have trip kings. I'd stay in for another card.

Around the table, cards were flipped and Pin drew a king. It paired him on the table. He was exuberant.

"Fold boys! Fold while you can!"

I drew a ten of spades, which gave me two pair—the dead man's hand. But unless I'd misread the table, I still had the edge on Pin. He was bluffing—absolutely going to try and muscle his way in and take the pot.

Wart, with trips on the table, bet. He was called and then raised heavily by Pin and in turn raised by Vegas, called and then raised by me. It was the first time Pin had actually paid attention to anyone other than himself and now he was forced to match the raises or fold. He stayed.

The pot was staggering for our normal sloppy Friday-night poker game. Stite was the only one who had sense enough to fold. There were still six of us in the game. Pin gave himself away. He had a slight tic. Whenever he was uncertain about his cards, he'd clench his teeth so tightly his jaw muscles would flex and pulse.

The next card was down and I drew the ace of diamonds, which gave me a full boat. I could not see anything that would beat aces and tens on the table, so I bet the max. I was in the perfect spot at the table. Pin should have dropped out but I'd gotten under his skin.

"What do you think you've got going, Metty?" he snarled.

"Pay to play, Pin. Pay to play." I remained calm and that incensed him.

"Two pair is a dead man's hand," he said, laughing. For a moment he hesitated and then called the bet. "Looking for a boat on the final card. It better be a life boat."

The players all laughed and I just nodded. The final card down caught me by complete surprise. Never in my life, before or since that night, have I ever had such a hand. It was an ace of hearts. Four honest aces, three of them down.

When my turn to bet came, I matched the pot. Chatter at the table stopped and those players still in looked carefully, probably for the first time, at my hand. A pot raise was a big deal. "I don't know what you've got down, Metty, but it's too rich for my blood," Wart said and flipped his cards over. Pin was the only player left on the table. The tension was thick. Pin could never have imagined what I had underneath; the odds were too astronomical.

"How much we got in the pot?" he asked, looking at about five dollars' worth of chips in his own stack.

"One hundred twenty-three dollars and change," Stite said, and then added—because he wasn't particularly fond of Pin either—"Pay attention, asshole."

"Are you folding?" I asked, so measured that I was positive I'd tipped him off.

"What do you have?" he asked, just as polite and casual as one might ask a stranger for the time of day.

"I have four of the most beautiful aces you've ever seen and three of them are down under." That was all it took.

"Four aces! My big, fat ass you do! I'll call."

"Match the pot," Vegas said.

"I'm going to have to go light," Pin replied.

"We don't play that way and you know it," Stite said. "Either put the money down or Metcalf takes the pot."

"I'm short on cash." There wasn't a sympathetic smile at the table.

I didn't want Pin to fold. I wanted him to see those cards but I couldn't let him go light because I'd never see the money.

"I don't have the cash right now. What if I put up a hundred and twenty-five dollars' worth of sports equipment?" he asked.

"Like what?"

"A West Yellowstone fly rod, a Shakespeare reel, a vest with some flies, and a pair of Red Ball waders."

"That don't make it," Stite said.

"Fuck you. It's up to Metcalf. It ain't up to you."

"That'll do," I said because fuses were getting short. "But you got to go get the gear."

"I'm not going to need to," he said.

"You will. And if you don't, the game is over."

"Are you serious? You want me to go down to my room and bring the gear back up so I can turn around and take it back down? Are you out of your mind?"

Pin slid his cards to Vegas to watch while he retrieved his fishing kit. When he returned he threw the gear into the corner. "There you go. I call."

I turned my cards over exactly as they had been dealt to me. At the full boat, the boys went wild. Aces and tens.

"That's a great hand," Stite said, clapping me on the back. "I'm glad I jumped ship when I did!"

Pin didn't say a thing for a few moments and then said, "What's the seventh card?"

"I told you already. It's an ace. Trust me, you don't want to see it."

"Turn the card over. I paid to see it."

When I did, Pin lunged over the table at me. He took a wild swing at me but was off-balance. The boys jumped on him and kept us separated. I did not relish mixing it up with Pin. He outweighed me by at least forty pounds and was a good six inches taller.

The game broke up and I took the gear to my room, where I stashed it in the closet. I went into the bathroom to brush my teeth before turning in, and Burr was standing at one of the sinks, shaving.

"I just had the poker hand of my life," I offered awkwardly. "Four aces, three down. Kicked Pin's ass."

Burr wasn't partial to Pin's privileged attitude so I thought this tidbit might get a smile out of him. Perhaps a snatch of conversation. Instead, he wiped the lather from his face, picked up his dock kit, and walked right by me as though I didn't exist.

ADDICTED

Just so it is understood clearly, I am an addict and it is difficult to see any possibility of recovery on the horizon. How can one surrender to a higher power when what one is addicted to is itself a higher power? I am addicted to fly-fishing and doubly addicted to the fish porn that attends to this addiction. Muscular bonefish in Belize, exotic permit, shark, stripers, fat Argentinean brown trout, steelhead, blue fin, wild Alaskan salmon, barracuda, and virtually anything that can be caught with a fly rod occupies my attention deep into the night and long after the civilized world has gone to sleep.

Unbeknownst to her, my wife, Alana, is an enabler of the first order, and the unsavory company I keep are of no help because they are also addicts. Bear with me. I place in front of the reader the following circumstances and leave you all to be the judge: guilty or not, black or white. To paraphrase Johnnie Cochran's infamous defense of O.J. Simpson, "If it doesn't fit, you must acquit," I offer my own argument for the case against total honesty in dealing with and excusing my disease: "If there is any gray, it must be okay."

1. All my fly rods are Winston "green sticks" in green aluminum tubes, but if Alana notices a new rod and asks, "Is that another fly rod?" I seize the moment with a reply that contains, at its core, a truth tied to an avoidance and a compliment. "Of course, honey, it's another fly rod and I tried to sneak it by you without notice." It might be a delusional rationale of sorts but "everybody" wins in this exchange. Yes?

2. I have lied to my employers shamelessly in the pursuit of trout and I have done so without regret. This is not easy to admit in such a public forum but the cardinal rules of a 12-step program require this. During the course of forty-two years of teaching, when a good run is on or a thick hatch manifests itself or the steelhead run on the Salmon River begins, I am taken by the disease's fevered pitch, so deliriously affected I have simply told lies about my whereabouts. I call these days "mental floss" days, a way of keeping my sanity by being on the water. I realize this is a personality flaw, a big one, so somewhere along the line I decided that the next time I was put in such a position, I would tell the truth—point blank. Let the cards fall where they might, so to speak.

3. Following one of the rare moments when I attended an actual faculty meeting, my department chair cornered me to mention that I rarely, if ever, attended these meetings and fellow faculty took it as a sign that I was aloof and standoffish. Furthermore, it was part of my contractual obligation, and he strongly recommended (bordering on insisted) that I be at the final faculty meeting.

What I wanted to say was that my main objection was that these were not, by any stretch of the imagination, meetings. For the most part they were lectures, and I don't do well with authority that tends to lecture my colleagues, who are dedicated educators. But in the interest of stopping myself from saying something I would most certainly regret, I instead said I would be at the final meeting. I think, truly, that I meant it.

Failure did not happen because of my disease. I don't exaggerate here: The morning of the final faculty meeting, I was on my way to campus, which coincidentally happened to be in the same general direction as the Provo River, when my car unexpectedly and inexplicably began veering slightly toward the south, along the angle of difference in that general direction. Toyota has had its share of problems with throttles that stick open, leaving the driver with little control in maintaining the speed and trajectory of the vehicle. I feared that might be true as well of my Subaru, so I didn't fight it. Next thing I knew, I ended up on the river in a seriously wicked midge hatch surrounded by angry brown trout.

I didn't feel particularly bad about missing the faculty meeting. I knew if I could manage to get past the next three days without seeing my department chair, we would both be into the summer and all would eventually be forgotten. I was unexpectedly put to the test though. There is an elevator in our building that I seldom use. But following such a day of fishing, I was a bit knackered and needed the lift. I saw the chair coming toward me and quickly tried to hit the *door close* button before he could get into the elevator. Instead I kept banging away on the *door open* button.

"Third floor?" I asked stupidly.

"Yes," he replied, seeming a bit confused by such an idiotic question. We both officed on the same floor, not many doors away from each other.

"You weren't at the meeting," he said.

"I know."

There was a long and painful pause. I took a deep breath and offered up the truth.

"I went fly-fishing."

He regarded me carefully, uncertain what to make of my comment. I offered nothing else. I'd put the truth out there and I would take whatever consequences it brought. Finally, after studying my sunburned face, noticing the white, tell-tale signs of polarized glasses, known to skiers and fishermen who spend a great deal of time outdoors as "raccoon eyes," he simply said, "Radiation?" Then he paused and said, "I hope it's successful."

A bigger man might have said, "No, actually I completed my rounds of radiation three weeks ago. I really went fly-fishing." But I

am not that man. That man is not me, particularly when the truth—
and we are talking about the call of trout—can set you free.

A NEAR-PERFECT DAY

It was my great friend Kranes who first introduced me to the Price River in the Wasatch Plateau, which flows eastward until it spills into the Green River. I'd heard about the wild brown, cutthroat, and rainbow trout for many years, but like many anglers I'd dismissed the river because of the drive time and the rumor that the water was unpredictable, muddy, and difficult to fish. It's a rumor that I still selfishly perpetuate today.

To get to the Price River required a two-hour drive from Salt Lake City, and once Kranes and I arrived we'd have to trespass onto property owned by the Denver and Rio Grande Railroad Company. This part of the equation appealed to me the most. In the pretzel logic of my fly-fishing mind, private water surrounded by public land should have some sort of access for all fishermen. Though many states have implemented carefully thought-out access rights, negotiated with landowners and legislators, Utah is not one of these enlightened states. In short, our pilgrimage onto the Price would be, as I imagined, an act of troutivism.

The Price River proved to be every bit as good as Kranes had promised. It's a meandering river that unfolds, in many ways, like a smaller and less trafficked version of Idaho's Silver Creek. All day long we caught wonderfully healthy brown trout along serpentine stretches of grassy banks using a variety of flies to match the changing hatch conditions of the day. Soon the Price would be the river we'd scramble to when our teaching schedules allowed us to fish together.

On one such fall day, we arrived earlier than usual and made our way along the river. Pale morning duns flittered in the cool early light, and trout were rising consistently and lazily to the fly. As was our custom, we divided the river in half, with Kranes taking the lower stretch while I worked the upper. He carried our rod cases and lunch to the meadow where we might meet for lunch if either of us could make ourselves step out of the water.

As he disappeared around the first bend in the river, I took inventory of the water. The beat I decided to fish was rather narrow, a series of almost perfect *S* curves with ample refuge for trout to hang on the lip of the river, protected from prey by overlapping grass. I took time to tie on a new tapered leader and go through my fly boxes. I pulled a dozen or so PMDs out and stuck them into my hat so I would waste little time once I began to cast.

Fall is my season, and I thought how fortunate to have these waters in my own backyard. What stands, I hope, in writing about wild places is not so much the exaggerated, perhaps overwritten or underwritten heroics of trout, but a more reflective examination of self. I belong to water.

Four brown trout began to feed in a measured pattern. They were spaced equally enough apart that it might be possible to land the lower trout first and, if luck and accurate casting prevailed, catch each successive trout without scattering the others. On my first cast, the fly disappeared and the brown took to fast water. I was fortunate enough to keep it below the others and landed it with relative ease. It was the same with the other three trout. The morning began with good fortune and continued as such. If there was a heaven, I would like it to be like this: a broad sweep of mountains cradling a beguiling stream laden with trout. Oh such dreams...what else would be required? I hoped my friend was having such a morning.

In rare moments on the river, time floats and slows to an immeasurable rhythm. The landscape of mountains and rounded hills dissolves into the river. It is all one can see: the narrow window of trout on water. Such is the hypnotic power of trout.

By the time I reached our rendezvous spot, Kranes was sitting comfortably on the bank, his feet hanging in the water, having lunch. I would not disclose how my morning with trout had unfolded until I heard of his day. He waved to me and I could see a broad smile across his face.

"My god, Metcalf, what a day! Never better." It was the truth. I grabbed a sandwich, opened a cold beer, and sat by him. We talked of the trout and the unusually good fortune that befell us this day. Perhaps at this moment we should have left the water, accepting this bounty as it were, as a flawless gift from the trout gods. I had never had such a day on my home waters before and knew just as certainly it could not end this way. I had not missed a single trout all day. Thirty-five landed and released without the unbuttoning of even one. I found it peculiar that on this day I was counting trout because I had given this folly up some thirty years ago. A day on the river was either a "good day," "a great day," or an "unbelievable day."

Because there was still a good half day in front of us, I decided I would walk the mile and a half back toward the car and fish to one more trout that I had marked carefully as we descended from the railroad tracks and onto the footpath. I did not stop to cast to this brown earlier in the day because the cast was impossibly difficult. The water was covered in a dense blanket of watercress with the exception of a twelve-inch path that went from the far side of the bank out into moving water. The railroad tracks were no more than twenty feet from where I would need to place myself for any kind of cast. I would have to enter into the watercress, slightly left of center, and shoot a long cast that landed to the right tip of the opening. If I missed on the first cast, it would be over. Too far left or right and my fly would snag up on the watercress. And in the event that I could make an absolutely perfect cast and the brown took the fly, it would immediately cut into the thick muck of vegetation and snap me off or, worse, be wrapped in such a fashion that it might drown. What did this say about me?

I sat down on a rock, tied on a new tippet, selected a flying ant, ginked it properly, and studied the brown's eating pattern. It wasn't difficult to understand how it had gotten so big and why it hung where it did. All advantage was to the brown. It had absolute protection, a bounteous food supply, and in the event a fly fisherman was able to stick it, it would be an easy enough escape. My fly rod was a 2-weight, 6' Orvis with a Battenkill reel. The drag was minimal and the cast had to be long and precise.

A voice whispered to me softly, "*Leave it alone Metcalf. You don't stand a chance.*" But another voice, more seductive and compelling, begged me to make the cast. It was the voice I listened to and have always regarded when trying to decide if I should make *just one more cast.* It is the voice that suggests ten more casts that easily become one hundred, or that makes me late for a dinner or cocktail party, or forget to go to work or pay bills or return phone calls. Its power over me is absolute.

It was a perfect cast and the brown slammed the fly. Instead of going into the weeds and watercress as I suspected it would, it slashed to the deep open current, where it pulled heavily on the rod. I played the trout, not knowing what else to do, and then it slowly began to move toward safe haven. Against everything I knew, I horsed the fish, hoping to somehow bring it up the slot and land it. It came toward me and I backed up the hill, trying to gain additional leverage.

What happened next is a faint blur. I slipped, lost my footing on the steep shale slope, and crashed to the ground without bracing my fall. I felt a sharp and painful bash to the head and blacked out. When I came to, my head was splitting. The rod was still clenched to my hand and I sat up slowly. I saw white stars and felt a split water bottle wet against my back. A train sounded and the ground rumbled. I attempted to stand up because I was perilously close to the tracks. I couldn't. An afternoon coal run on the Denver and Rio Grande blasted its horn and rolled past me, blasting its whistle. I reached back with my hand and touched the water on my neck. It was blood.

I went to retrieve my fly line when it gave a tug, and the trout began to move slowly up the channel. Miraculously my rod had not been broken in the fall, and the trout was still on the fly. I pushed my hand to the gash on my head and reeled with my teeth until I was able to slide down the slope and land the brown. I carefully lifted the trout from the water and reached down to unhook it. I plunged my hands into the water and blood from my hand washed a ghostly film over the water. The trout was spent so I carefully cradled it and massaged it, working it gently until it gained its strength and disappeared.

I took stock of my situation. My head was bleeding steadily and I had a blinding headache that suggested I might have a concussion. To muddle matters, I was two hours from any emergency clinic and a three-mile walk to collect Kranes and return back to the road. I knew I couldn't make the distance. I was shaky and unbalanced. I had an emergency first-aid kit in my SUV, and I could use the side mirrors to see exactly what I'd done to myself, so I headed back to the rig.

Coming toward me was another fly fisherman. From his angle he couldn't see the cut side of my head. As he approached he greeted me. "How's it going?"

"A terrific PMD hatch, a few caddis beginning to appear on the water."

When he got closer he saw my head. "Jesus Christ, are you okay?" He looked alarmed. "What happened? You should see a doctor."

"Yes," I said.

I'd seen him on the water before and we'd chatted about fishing but I could see that he was nervous.

"Are you headed downstream?" I asked, attempting to convince him that I was indeed okay.

"Yes."

"I wonder if I could ask a favor."

"Of course."

"I'm fishing with a friend. I think you've seen him with me before. He's about a mile and a half downriver. Maybe more. He's the only one on the river. His name is Kranes. David. Would you let him know that I bashed my head pretty good and I need to get to an emergency room?"

"Of course," and then he asked me again, "Are you certain you're okay?"

"I think so."

When I opened the back of my rig a gust of hot air blasted my face and I vomited bile. I couldn't find my first-aid kit and then remembered I'd taken it out during a cleaning and not replaced it. In the mirror I could see the cut clearly, blood caked down my neck and dried deep crimson stains on my shirt. Medically sound or not, I tore a strip of duct tape and closed the gap on my head. I then plastered a strip from the top of my hat over my ears and the frame of my glasses. My head was throbbing. I sat on the back bumper and sipped some water. The rig was exposed to the sun, and I thought it best to get back to the river, where I could at least splash some cold water on my face and wait.

I started to lock the rig and decided that if I was going to die here because of some internal hemorrhaging I might as well take my fly rod and fish until Kranes arrived. I snipped off my fly and put on a small caddis and began to cast along the banks. My casts were surprisingly clean. At least I thought so. While I fished, I thought how this was a perfect place to die. I felt strangely at peace with the idea. Not by a heart attack at the symphony or walking to class, but here on a river that produced beautiful, angry fish, making a cast into the hope and promise of another trout. Every cast, I thought,

has as part of its delivery "possibility." I can only speak for myself—
though I imagine I am not the first to consider this idea—but I
always believe, often against all odds, that there will be another fish
at the end of the fly.

An hour passed before I heard Kranes calling to me. I waved
to him and got out of the water to meet him.

"My god, Metcalf, what happened?"

"I split my head open trying to land a fish. I need to get to an
emergency room. Soon. Can you drive?"

"I don't think so," he replied. "I'm a bit lightheaded."

"Then I'll drive, but keep your eyes on me."

"Okay."

At the top of Soldier Summit there is a little gas station and
convenience store. I told Kranes I needed to get something cold to
drink and offered to get him something. I stepped into the store and
headed to the back cooler to grab a couple of cold waters. When
I took them up to the front the young cashier, who was in his late
teens or early twenties, took one look at me and said, "Just take
them. I don't want any trouble."

"Pardon me?" I replied. "Why would I do something like that?"

"We got robbed here last night and we don't need any more
trouble."

He was staring at the caked blood on the side of my head and
on my shirt. "No. No. That's not necessary. I got banged up landing
a fish."

"Seriously. Just take 'em and go."

"I can't." I took a fiver from my wallet and put it on the counter
and left.

"You got change coming, Mister."

"Keep it."

I WASN'T KEPT waiting long at the emergency room. By the time
I got into a space, the doc came in to take a look at me. An ER nurse

was cleaning up the side of my face and just beginning to try and take off the duct tape without ripping off my sideburns and a chunk of hair. The doctor started to laugh.

"It's the first time I've ever seen anything like this before. The duct tape. Inventive."

"Thanks. Best I could do under the circumstances." I liked him.

"I've got a serious question to ask."

"Go ahead, ask away."

"How was the fly-fishing?"

"Great. Actually, fantastic." And because I was curious, "How'd you know?"

"Flies stuck in the side of your hat."

"Right."

"Where'd you go?"

"Price River."

"One of my favorite little rivers."

"You fly-fish?"

"Yes, but never enough."

"Never is."

The doc bantered with me the entire time as he cleaned and stitched me up. In between talking about fishing, he asked a series of medical questions and took some x-rays, just to make certain I didn't have any serious internal damage. While Kranes sat in the waiting room, I waited for them to study the findings. I started to doze off when the doc came back into the room.

"You're going to live," he said, leaving the room for a minute while the nurse walked me through a list of warning symptoms I needed to be aware of in case I *did* have a concussion.

"And call us if you show any of these signs. The number is on the bottom, and we have doctors here twenty-four hours a day."

The doctor returned and handed me his card. "This is my direct number. Call me if you have any concerns, okay?"

"Okay. And thanks. Thank you very much."

"You're very welcome." There was a slight pause and then he added, "Maybe I'll see you on the river one day."

"That would be my great pleasure, Doc." We shook hands, and I left to collect Kranes and go home to my wife and family.

ONE MIGHT SUSPECT a calamity like this would not be wasted on me. Perhaps, instead of listening to the voice that encourages me to try the improbable, wade in risky waters, fish beyond my ability, and place myself in the path of danger, I could consider the experience on the Price River as a prophecy of things to come if I did not mend my ways. But how can one fly-fish partially, be of two worlds—the world of caution *and* the world of the wild? It is not possible for me, and I must meet the water on its own terms.

COCKTAIL

Kranes and I have fished together for more years than either of us can remember. We survived the wild days of drinking hard, fishing hard, forgetting to eat, eating to forget, forgetting to call home— often sharing a small cabin on the Salmon River several falls in a row. Once, after a long and productive day of fly-fishing and a for-gettable dinner, Kranes concocted a new drink for us to celebrate the Salmon. We sat outside on the deck, listening to the symphony of rock over water and drinking until the canyon walls slanted in a greenish-blue sigh, elk two hundred strong bugling into the sky in a sacred chorus of stories. It was a powerful drink made from what-ever alcohol or rocket fuel Kranes had brought back from a recent trip to Romania or the planet Mars, and it lit us up pretty good. Straight up, in a thousand years we could never re-create the cock-tail or the dream seam it spun around us both that night.

In the morning I put on the coffee pot and attempted to unscramble the dream, to focus the lens, sharpen the image, but it was wild...some sort of hot sex with a woman or an alien who could sing the blues and coax fish up from the Salmon River. It's true; this is not a work of fiction.

I sat on the front deck, fog vapors lifting off the river, the light stretching itself across the canyon walls, lazy and slow. How would I talk to Kranes about this? I wanted to say something because I was afraid I might have howled in the night. It was a dream of talons and flesh.

Kranes grabbed his coffee and padded out onto the deck. He looked scattered, more so than he usually did. He sat down facing the river and looked across it at the sweeping landscape, the upper mountains dusted in light October snow. "You'll never believe the dream I had last night," he began, "it was like none I've ever had before."

"Me too!" I replied, adding sheepishly, "It was an ungodly dream."

We spent the better part of the morning engaged in a deciphering of and a speculation on these dreams before we took off for an afternoon of fly-fishing up Yankee Fork. That night, worn by the hiking and pushing water, we settled back into the cabin and built some cocktails that we hoped would take us to the same place. We did not speak directly of the hope of dream catching again, but drank in the hope of inviting whatever muse had visited us to come back. In the end, both our dreams that night were uneventful and pedestrian.

If the dreams did not come from the alcohol, were they of our own secret landscapes of desire? What forces might have been in place at the confluence of wild water and a wilderness that so permeated our dreams, and rendered us hungry, hot, and barbaric? It is just *that*, I have come to understand; the unexpected and unexplainable that always draws me back to water over and over again.

MERMAID

————

The summer of 1978 began rough enough. I was down and out.
Literally. I was down because I was going through a contentious
divorce, and I was out because I was out of the house and sleeping
on the couch of my good friend and fly-fishing buddy BT. Although
he would never say anything, and perhaps because of my fear of
imposing on others, I felt like I was crowding him and needed to
find other lodging.

The summer was nearly on me and if I could make it through
the last quarter of teaching I could lay a summer plan that might
save my life. My soon-to-be ex-wife had just completed law school,
and I offered her the house so there could be some sort of grounding
for her while she studied for the bar. I took very little with me: four
boxes of books, enough clothes to get by until I could find a place
of my own, and all my fly-fishing gear. The rest could be retrieved
when I returned from wherever it was I was headed for the summer
months. That was part of the problem. I had no sense of place or
destination. For the first time in many years, I was a man without
a landscape.

By good fortune, in a conversation with a friend who worked
for the Department of Lands for the State of Idaho, I discovered
that if I filed gold-mining claims on any stretch of river in Idaho,
I could live on the property. Not many people filed claims and not
much was required to fulfill the state's requirements.

I pored over topographic maps, focused on the Salmon River.
The process was simple. A claim needed to be registered; the property line clearly staked out and recorded with the Department of

Lands. Other than that, nothing much was required, and if there were no other claims on the property I could set up camp and live there for as long as the claim was active.

My claims ran for several miles along the Salmon River just outside of Stanley, Idaho, heading toward Challis. I selected that stretch of river because I knew that area and there was good access to trout and several natural hot springs. My base camp was a spot on the river across Rough Creek Bridge, on a flat stretch of land. A large, flat granite boulder served as my kitchen and there was ample space to pitch a tent. Large fir trees offered shade during the day and broke the canyon winds at night. I dug a fire pit and layered it with river rock. I foraged around an old mining site on the property and found a rusted box spring that would serve as a grill. Two days of hard work and I'd managed to set up a comfortable base. A home for the summer.

I fired up my pipe and thought what a great country it was where a man could live on a beautiful river full of trout and wake up every morning to the damp smell of pine and the babbling of a river.

It was here, in the bosom of this wild landscape, where I cooked trout wrapped in aluminum foil, drizzled in butter, stuffed with lemon and garlic salt and garnished with wild onion, with a spud roasting in the coals for my supper. It was here, in the rolling hills heading toward Loman, where I was taught where to pick wild morel mushrooms.

Within a week of arriving in Stanley—after fly-fishing daily, reading, writing, soaking in hot springs, and driving into town at night to drink and dance at Casanova Jack's Rod and Gun Club, the Plywood Palace, or the Kasino Club—I began to heal.

I disappeared almost completely that summer. For many reasons, neither my wife nor I had spoken about our impending divorce. In part, I imagine, because we had been considered to be the "perfect couple" and because, although we both sensed the damage was irreparable, it felt like we had failed each other. My wife needed "space," and I knew what this meant. I told her that if I left I would never return. We'd gotten married young and struggled to put each other through college. We fell away from each other and, to be brutally honest, we put very little effort into salvaging the relationship. The damage was already done.

I did not make a single phone call to anybody during the month of June. I spent July Fourth in Stanley, sitting in a chair on Ace of Diamonds Street along with the local townspeople, watching the fireworks explode on top of Nip and Tuck Mountain. Following the fireworks, I retired to Casanova Jack's to dance with some of the women who had come up from Sun Valley for the weekend. That night the Braun Brothers were playing, and I danced until the bar closed. Just before driving back to Rough Creek, drunk on the evening, I called Todd Smith, an old friend from Evergreen, Colorado, and invited him to come fly-fishing and camp with me. And a week later, Smitty, Lenz, and Saling—all miscreants and devout fishermen—arrived from Colorado loaded for whatever mischief came their way.

Nothing was required or expected on any given day. We'd often have a lazy breakfast of eggs, bacon, and hash browns, then head off to catch trout, gut and clean them, and store them in a cooler for dinner. In the evenings we'd submerge ourselves in some hot springs I'd discovered off the beaten tracks, then dress up in our finery and head into town to drink, play pool, and country swing until the wee hours of the morning.

Following one such night, when we had clearly drunk too much whiskey and almost got into a brawl with a bunch of local cowboys who felt we were homing in on their dates, we were tossed from the bar by the local cops. In no uncertain terms we were told to leave Stanley and that if the cops spotted us again, we'd be arrested. We walked across the street and headed into the Plywood Palace, where against our better judgment we continued drinking and dancing. It was not a good decision.

The next morning, around the camp in various configurations of bent and curled bodies, I found the boys, half in their sleeping bags, face down in the dirt. Once we got some coffee in us and took a cold plunge in the Salmon, the boys decided to head downriver to pick on some trout. It was sheer bravado, but I could not muster up such a false front to join them. When they disappeared, I crawled back into the tent and quickly fell asleep.

Midday, I awoke and built myself a cold trout sandwich and washed it down with a beer. Thank god the sky was overcast or I would have melted. Even with the cold river plunge earlier in the day, I was hurting and reeked of whiskey. I grabbed my fly rod and a dozen reliable flies, and headed off to a spot that I knew wouldn't be heavily fished. The spot was not far from a campground, and it was well hidden from the road. And although campers were beginning to show up for the tourist season, I was fairly certain I'd be alone on the water. I parked on the highway and dropped down a steep scrabble-rock incline until I hit the water. I would fish a quarter-of-a-mile stretch until I entered into a nearby campground and then walk or hitchhike back to the car.

I tied on a small Parachute Adams and started casting to some trout in a back eddy that were carelessly slurping from the foam seam. Within the first few casts, I managed to land a few decent-sized trout that I tucked into my creel and released the rest. By late afternoon I was in much better spirits and began to feel almost human again. Two bends away from the campground was when I first spotted the mermaid. She stopped me cold. Retreating from the river, I climbed to the bank and studied her.

Sitting in the water in a lawn chair ten feet from the shore, completely naked and reading a paperback novel, was a beautiful woman. I guessed her to be roughly my age. She was deeply tanned and wore a red bandana pulled back that held her auburn hair in a wild bunch. I watched her for some time, trying to imagine how I could get around her without revealing myself. I couldn't climb out of the canyon and make my way back to the road because the cliffs were too sheer. And sure as hell I couldn't exactly avoid her without making a fool out of myself. I would have to walk almost directly up to her, apologize profusely, and side skirt my way into the campground and then back onto the highway. None of these options could be done discreetly. Instead, I sat on a rock and regarded her with envy. I came to admire how completely relaxed she was in her nakedness in the natural world. I tried to imagine what circumstance had placed her here, on the Salmon River at just this point in her life. Was she a refugee from a failed marriage? Recouping from a broken relationship by bathing herself in the holy water of the Salmon? After all, it was exactly what I was doing. Finally, I elected to fish my way up to her, keeping my eyes on the water and then feigning surprise if she was still there when I arrived. This option offered her the possibility of gracefully exiting the river and returning to her campsite without notice.

The plan did not work. Though I kept my head down and caught and released a few more trout, every time I looked up from the water to mark her whereabouts on the river, she was still sitting undisturbed. As I closed the gap between us I looked up and noticed she was watching me. She waved at me and I clumsily waved back at her. At that point, there was no longer any reason to pretend I hadn't seen her so I hooked my fly into the butt section of my handle and, as delicately as I could, made my way toward her. I tried desperately to think of something clever to say but words failed me miserably. What can one possibly say to a naked woman sitting in a river?

"You've got a beautiful cast," she said, smiling broadly at me.

"Thank you," I mumbled, and added stupidly, "and you ..."

"And I am a naked woman in the Salmon River," she replied, laughing at my sentence that could not be completed.

"Yes."

"If you could cook the way you cast, I'd run off with you in a minute."

"I can cook."

"Really? Well then, how would you feel about cooking for me tonight?"

"I'd like that very much."

"Good. Are you staying in the campground?" She got up from the chair, tucked the book under her chin, and made her way over to the bank.

"If you'd like, I can take the chair."

"Thank you. I'm fine."

Folded neatly on a weathered log were a pair of faded Levi's, a white western shirt, a cowboy hat, and a pair of cowboy boots. I turned my back while she got dressed.

"Where are you camped?" she asked.

"About two miles downriver, on Rough Creek," I replied, glancing back to see if she'd completed getting dressed. "My rig is on the road about half of a mile from here."

"Do you need a ride?"

"No, thank you. I can walk or hitch a ride. Somebody always stops."

"Don't be silly. We can take my truck. It's no problem."

"Are you sure?"

"I wouldn't have offered."

We walked back to her campsite. She had a beautiful camper that she towed behind a pickup truck. The truck was a maroon Ford, relatively new. When we got inside the cab, she introduced herself. Her name was Karen. In turn, I introduced myself. When she dropped me off, we set a time and I promised to return with all the trappings for a trout dinner.

Driving back toward Rough Creek I had a difficult time wrapping my head around what had transpired. Things like this seldom happened to me. Actually, things like finding a beautiful naked woman in the Salmon River and being asked to dinner never happened to anyone, at least nobody I knew.

The boys, on the other hand, presented a problem for me. I worried there would be no way to get away from them but when I pulled up to the camp, they were nowhere to be found. I quickly scribbled a note telling them I wouldn't be there for dinner. I lied and wrote that I had some mining business in Sun Valley and I wouldn't get home until late that night. Not wanting to have them come up on me while I was at camp, I grabbed a clean change of clothes, my toilet kit, and everything I'd need to cook dinner, and headed toward the Sunbeam Hot Springs to bathe.

Dinner with Karen was sublime, and we talked as though we had known each other for years. Her story was a straightforward narrative that included discovering that the man she loved and had lived with for the past eight years was, in fact, two-timing her. She worked as a finish carpenter. She was the only girl in a family of four boys, and she'd taken to woodworking with her father. At first it was a hobby, but she found passion in the work, feeling as though she was born to it. When she uncovered her boyfriend's tryst, she simply packed up everything that was important to her, left the house to her ex, and decided to head toward the open country of Montana. I liked how strong she was, how she detected problems in her life and made changes to ensure her survival. Her story spoke to me in a profound and meaningful way. What she had processed, almost instantly, offered me a different lens with which to look at my own situation. Sometimes in life things can't be fixed, and the sooner one realizes that the more unencumbered the path becomes. There was an undercurrent in her story that murmured, "Trust your instincts."

I spoke to her openly about my marriage, about my failures and my bewilderment that two people who had once been so in love with each other had so completely fallen apart. At the core of my voice and in the revealing nakedness of my own narrative I felt lighter. I felt an honesty and openness in her listening that was beyond judgment. In the unfolding events of the day, there was magic indeed— of the mermaid, the vision of a naked woman on the Salmon River, the sexual imagination of circumstance, and the ensuing unbridled honesty Karen embodied. She was, through her narrative, instructing me, and I paid attention.

It was getting late and although I wanted to spend the night with her I did not push the issue. So much could be lost in that moment, and it would change what I had already been offered. I could not press the night. I stood up from the campfire and thanked her for a wonderful evening.

"I probably should get going," I said.

"You don't need to," she replied, taking my hands and squeezing them gently. "I'd like you to stay with me tonight."

So I did.

THE SEAM

Before Max accepted the "gift" of fly-fishing, he was cocky, restless, unsettled, lost in his own skin, uncertain about the world and how he would fit into the grand scheme of things. *Anxious*—a better word. He was anxious. He felt of the lost generation. But below the surface, I felt Max understood something important. Out of all the students in my English class for "at-risk" students, I most felt this in him. There was a current.

Among other things, we read Hemingway. Max began to unlock the mysteries of literature. He understood and recognized something of himself in *The Sun Also Rises*. The characters' voices spoke to him, and the world of literature offered up a lifeline. He saw, in a certain profound way, that he was not alone. It was an important discovery.

What I liked about Max then was the slow boil, the unlocking of the mystery, the reading of a text and the conversion from the ethereal to the physical. I hoped and wished for him what Irish poet Seamus Heaney offers us in *The Cure at Troy*: "History says, Don't hope / On this side of the grave, / But then, once in a lifetime / The longed-for tidal wave / Of justice can rise up / And hope and history rhyme." Would this be enough? I wondered. Literature and open water.

When Max graduated from high school he promised to stay connected. "Seriously, man, I'll stay in touch. Wait and see. I'm going to go to college. Maybe teach." I didn't hold my breath. He was off and away. He had demons to wrestle with, energy to burn. If he did stay in touch with me or any of the teachers in our little school, it would be a wonderful thing. Just to know. Unfortunately, where I taught this didn't often happen. Life gets in the way. People move and disappear.

Over the years, I've come to realize that Max reminded me of myself at that age: a messed-up jigsaw puzzle looking for a little guidance. Mrs. Neilson and Mrs. Broadbent, my eleventh- and twelfth-grade English teachers, taught me how to read—how to go beneath the surface of the written word and find the human and personal connection. Along the way, others offered me help. Three college professors believed in me and we often fly-fished together. During university, fly-fishing kept me sane. Under their mentorship I became a teacher. I've remained in touch with all three of them for almost forty years. On occasion, when I can coax one of them out, we still fly-fish together.

Several years later, true to his word, Max found me again, and I was surprised. I invited him to my house for a scotch. While we drank, he talked. He'd gone off to college and had been kicked out for failing grades. A professor had intervened, spoke up on his behalf, and he was reinstated. He became a student. He graduated, married a beautiful woman he'd dated in high school, and then pursued a master's in fine arts. After obtaining his degree, he landed a teaching position at Arizona State University in the Department of English, where he taught for twelve years. I checked on him over the years through colleagues I'd worked with at literary conferences, and I always heard great things about his teaching and about the man he had become.

Whenever he returned to Salt Lake City for a visit, Max would telephone and we'd attempt, if time allowed, to rendezvous for a cup of coffee. On one such occasion, he told me he'd begun to fly-fish seriously. He spoke of Black River, the Salt River, Verde River, and of high mountain lakes on the Mogollon Rim in northern Arizona. Max spoke of these waters and trout with great respect and appreciation. I understood then that he had found the seam that would keep him connected to the wild in all the most important ways.

Our fortunes changed, and we both found ourselves teaching at the University of Utah in the English Department. We were finally able to see each other on a daily basis, and we began to fly-fish together. Soon, on the days that our schedules allowed, we would make our way to one of several rivers we have in our backyard.

One brilliantly cold and crisp winter morning we headed to the Middle Provo River to fish a stretch of water that had been kind to us on several occasions. The thermometer registered twenty-eight degrees, surprisingly cold considering how the sun was shining. I parked the car and we climbed out onto a frozen pasture. At that temperature, while we pulled our gear from the back of my car, our conversation dropped to minimal grunts and minor complaints. Our waders were cold and brittle; the boots, frozen from being left in the car, were difficult to lace. I found myself quietly asking, Why? At this temperature we both knew the fish would be stingy.

The walk to any river with a friend invites a ritualistic call and response. And although I knew what fly Max would tie to the end of his tapered leader, I still asked. "What are you going to use?"

"A streamer," he replied, his nostrils exhaling ghostly vapor. "You?"

"I don't know," I answered.

The truth, of course, is that Max knows I will probably look for knuckles in the water, pockets and little slips of river where browns might be sipping blue wings or midges. But at this moment, an answer is required.

"Something dry. I'll probably do some headhunting."

Max is always first onto the water. There is an absolute certainty about his thinking that can't be faulted. He selects streamers because he can go deep into fast water where big trout hold. Before I had even selected a fly, he was upriver casting and slipping into a second run. Occasionally I'd hear him curse and I'd see a blur of arm and line, measured and methodical. Soon he disappeared around a bend in the river, leaving me to my own thoughts.

Slowly I walked the bank studying the water and looking for the occasional rise. Almost an hour later, in surprisingly shallow water on the bend of a corner where fast water slacked into slow, I saw the big-shoulder rise of a brown trout. Reaching up to my vest for gink, I was careful not to lose sight of this fish. The gink was cold and dense. It globbed onto my thumb and index finger where I worked it into liquid before applying it to a #26 Griffith's gnat.

Because of a particularly strange current, I preferred to be a bit closer before casting to this brown, but I knew better. On a day such as this, where at best I might be lucky to see half-a-dozen rises, I couldn't take the chance of spooking this trout. I began to false cast, letting out line until the fly was a couple feet upriver from the trout. I could see the tip of my line land delicately on the seam but immediately lost sight of the Griffith's gnat in the fold of water and shadows. I made several such casts and only once did the brown move toward what I suspected to be my fly. I set. Sloppily. The fly was nowhere near where I suspected it might be, and this realization made me laugh. Such a careless lift from the water made me check my cast. I held off for the moment and looked away from the trout to rest my eyes. A bald eagle, perched in a bleached-out cottonwood, watched me closely.

Much of the morning went this way: a few casts to the rising trout before I would back off and wait. It is a ritualistic dance I have come to know and love in the most profound way. All of life here on the water a joyous and comical dance full of promise and marginal successes. I knew full well that the possibility of landing the trout on a tiny Griffith's gnat, almost imperceptible to my eye, was a fool's folly. And yet it was the way I cared to spend this winter morning. In this regard, Max and I are very different in the way we approach fly-fishing.

When the trout finally slurped the gnat, I was prepared. This time I set properly and the water exploded. For a brief second, the trout was on, dove violently into the deeps and snapped me off.

I found Max working a riffle, casting into foamy swirling water. For a while I just watched him work the water. To the left of where he cast, a small, narrow island split the water with some terrific spots where trout could hold in relative safety. And directly at the head of the island sat a deep spring that fed a channel where we both knew there were substantial brown trout. It is a perfect spot because both sides are covered with thick, wild brush and the depth of the water offers protection without affording predators a safe vantage point to perch. Even in the winter, with the leaves stripped off all the branches, the potential to hang a fly on an overhanging limb is high. Because of this, many anglers make a few half-hearted casts and move upriver to water that is more forgiving. It is perfect streamer water and ideally suited to Max's style.

Max greeted me with a wave of his rod. "Any luck?"

"I hooked one, but it unbuttoned me," I replied. "You?"

"I've caught some decent fish."

"Did you try the channel?" I asked, nodding my head toward the slot.

"Hooked a big one twice but I can't keep him on. He's crafty."

"I'd expect as much."

After a moment, he suggested that I give it a try. "Go ahead, cast," he directed me. "Let me see how the master does it."

"I'm set up for dries."

"Take my rod, it has a streamer on it."

"You're left-handed."

Max sensed I was uncomfortable stepping into a stretch he'd been fishing.

"Come on, please," he beckoned. "I've been holding the spot for you."

"Max, seriously, I'm comfortable watching you."

"You would give me the spot, wouldn't you?"

"Of course," I replied.

"I'm just doing the same."

The gesture went beyond a mere trout. I took his rod and cast, and let go of the streamer into the waning light of the morning— across the history of our friendship and into the deepening darkness of the future.

The brown I landed was indeed a gift, but even more enduring is the memory of a young Max, going from high school to college, promising to stay in touch with me and doing so. That is more beautiful than any fish I can ever catch, and I've appreciated it deeply.

DEATH SONG

For the last several years I have had the luxury of spending a couple of weeks each June at a friend's ranch in Stanley, Idaho. During the first week my entire family joins me and we eat, drink, play horseshoes, catch up on each other's lives, visit with old friends, hang out at Red Fish Lake, and bathe in the exquisite light of the Sawtooth Mountains. And we always fly-fish together, casting to floating hot dogs, hatchery fish that are stocked in many of the dredge ponds up Yankee Fork. It is easy fishing and although it is not necessarily my preference in fly-fishing, it is a treat to watch my son and son-in-law iron out the kinks in their casting and land fish. With each fish landed and released a sort of calm takes them over and they seem at home.

The ponds are gorgeous, deep blue-green, in part, I suspect, from the irreparable damage of relentless dredge mining during the gold-mining boom of the mid-1800s. At the top of Yankee Fork a mammoth gold-mining dredge is landlocked and remains as a historical reminder of what we have done to the landscape. It is a dinosaur that clawed its way up the canyon and spit out giant boulders for a five-mile stretch, leaving the land scarred and sterile. It is a hideous *aide-memoire* to our reckless disregard of the natural world. It is a body scar that offers us a glimpse of the past and serves as a warning about the future.

When my family leaves Stanley, I am left alone for a week to work on my writing. The first day, the silence of my absent family is deafening. I get up at first light and try to sort things, to make sense of my life in the way I feel most honest. I write. I can't shake it and the process speaks to me, calls me out and makes me examine myself in a way that I can't do in the other world. I am carrying some heavy weight these days. At the end of this self-imposed ritual I will return home to begin a course of radiation targeted at a tumor on my liver. It is the fourth appearance of cancer in my body in nine years, and I am beat up mentally and physically. Fly-fishing and wild water are important elements in this battle against a savage and uncompromising disease, and they connect me to the *real* in a most absolute manner. I would be crippled without rivers and trout.

Earlier this week I'd noticed the appearance of salmon flies, thick and blanketed on the Salmon River. Fish were reckless in their feeding and since I was locked into an essay that was not cooperating, I grabbed my fly rod and made my way to the river. There is a small spot I like to fish, and I knew it held some good-sized cutthroat. Perhaps I could entice a trout or two onto a salmon fly. Before entering the water, I studied the river's narrative. Much is revealed to a fly fisherman in the first moments on any stretch of familiar or unfamiliar water. Fluctuations in the river change any body of water. That which might have been familiar a year before can be completely transformed a year later. Taking time to regard the water properly, looking for tongues and ripples, rings and slurps, makes up one part of an aesthetic. Water is where I needed to be.

It might have been a bit late in the day for the salmon fly hatch but it didn't stop me. Perhaps the trout had gorged themselves earlier and were off the fly. I tied on a salmon fly with a zebra midge as a dropper and began working upriver on the run I'd selected. I was meticulous about the presentation of the fly and paid close attention to its slightest drag. When it began to lose its buoyancy, I withdrew it from the water and dusted it with a silicon floatant. Rather haphazardly, trying to get the tapered leader and butt-end section of the fly line clean of the smallest guide, I made a short cast into water where no trout would ever hold. On perhaps my third or fourth cast the water exploded. It startled me completely and that seldom happens. It was a fat cutthroat, and it cartwheeled in a giant arc trying to unbutton the zebra midge. Instinctively it headed for deep water to use the current against the fly. I pursued it, tightening the drag of my reel and trying to stay upright in the water at the same time. I clearly had little control of the matter, and it pleased me to no end. When I started to get some line on my reel and felt the cutthroat slowing, it made one last hard run and headed for a large boulder midriver. I had to turn the cutthroat or I would lose him if he wrapped around the sharp, angular rock. My 6x tippet could snap. Suddenly the ripping stopped but my rod was still bent to the river. I knew the fish was still on the fly and that it had managed to wrap itself around the boulder or found some configuration that allowed respite from the threat of being caught. I dipped my rod down to the water, letting off the tension on the fly. This technique had worked before: the trout, feeling off the hook, would often bolt from grassy banks and make another run.

In a certain slant of light on the water, I got a glimpse: it was a fat and healthy-looking fish and was clearly wrapped around the boulder. It was equally apparent that I would not be able to dislodge it from its refuge. I quickly snapped my tippet off, leaving the cutthroat to the moment. When I did so, it did not blast off into the deeps as I expected but instead stayed anchored to the rock. Somehow, in its mad effort to escape, it had cinched itself tightly onto the rock. In vain it slashed against the current. I tried to find a way to get to the rock and break it off, but the water was too deep and dangerous for me to wade in. If it didn't break off soon, this marvelous, healthy, powerful cutthroat would drown.

Slowly the fish began to lose strength. It was my obligation to remain in the water and see this to the end, to offer a fish song and an apology for how the day would end. I suspect it was a surprise to us both. For some reason, I thought of two stanzas from a Theodore Roethke poem. The title escaped me, and I couldn't put the poem in any sort of context. I wondered perhaps if the lines had

surfaced at just the moment they needed to be summoned. I spoke
the words to the cutthroat:

Such owly pleasures! Fish come first, sweet bird.
Skin's the least of me. Kiss this.
Is the eternal near, fondling?
I hear the sound of hands.
Can the bones breathe? This grave has an ear.
It's still enough for the knock of a worm.
I feel more than a fish.
Ghost, come closer.

The river instructs and speaks to me in a tongue of gurgling
water and mystery. There are parallels to my own life. I know this
clearly. We are all born of water and what happens to us is uncertain. Let it remain so. I am prepared.

SPLIT SECOND

The winter of 2015 arrived late, and when spring arrived early the runoff in the Wasatch Mountains came hard and fast. The Provo River, the Weber River, and the Logan River were at their highest levels in over three decades. Under such circumstances, it makes for difficult fly-fishing—configuration of these rivers no longer familiar waters to me. Instead these waterways had been forced through nature to accommodate this turbulent flow and defined new geography, flooding farmland and devouring large cottonwood trees and thousands of tons of riverbank. It was thick and tempestuous water, chocolate and roiling, and only a madman would entertain the notion of casting a fly in such water.

These waters have been my home, and I fish them more than most. In truth, they have saved my life on more than a few occasions. I seek refuge in the quiet solitude of rivers, and in dark hours of my life—including this particular year—I need desperately to be fly-fishing.

For the past ten years I have been waging a very intense and personal war against an aggressive form of prostate cancer. I've spent more time in waiting rooms and doctors' offices than I would care to admit. My prognosis was disheartening, but I've managed to cheat the odds and survive well beyond medical expectations. I'm convinced this is in great part due to several factors: good medical attention, a fierce and often annoying trait I have of being a very vociferous advocate for my own health care, and finally, in no small measure, the absolute calm I feel in the press of water. This last element is by far the most important to me.

I don't fear death, I understand it. I fear burden and incapacitation more than I fear the end. But there is still the weight and anxiety of my disease, and I can keep this at bay by traveling to the river to wet a line.

This spring, my PSA numbers—a measure of my form of cancer—were at an alarming high. Since I'd already undergone a radical prostatectomy and eight long weeks of radiation, plus four other stints of radiation, clinical trials, and the brutal effects of continuous injections of a female hormone, it was discouraging news. My doctors were looking at their shoes, making references to promising protocols on the horizon, but after ten years of careful observation and solid research I knew the trajectory of things to come, and it was not particularly encouraging.

I was becoming anxious and snappy around my family, which is not my normal disposition, and I was not sleeping well. I would awaken deep into the night and find myself unable to go back to sleep. So as not to disturb my wife, I would pad into the study and read or find myself in the kitchen making stock and homemade soups. The kitchen is another way I keep my demons at arm's length, but even this diversion produced moderate results. So for the sake of my family and myself, it was essential to chase water.

Patrick Tovatt is a hopeless fishing slut like myself. It took a life-affirming conversion from alcohol and drugs to fly-fishing to clear his pipes. A former soap opera star, he spent twenty-five years with major television studios, and when he needed it most he found religion in fly-fishing. He surrendered himself to this higher order, and it saved his life.

The first time we ever fished together was almost three decades ago, and he was still drinking hard. When Tovatt stopped drinking and smoking he did it cold turkey. He took some of his "soap money" and purchased a beautiful place on New York's Beaverkill River, tied flies, and fished himself back to life. He's a tall, rugged man, athletic, muscular, and—even at seventy-two—he's not somebody you'd want to pick a fight with. A gritty guitar player with a twisted sense of humor, Tovatt recently cut a satirical album, *Plain & Nothing Fancy*, lambasting right-wing politicians, in particular the Bush "catastrophe." His music is an old-school throwback to yesteryear's political comedians, and he makes no apology for the unbridled lyrics. He protests for causes he believes in, kicks the people who kick the dog, and is unquestionably one of the most well-read people I've ever known. What I most appreciate about Tovatt is that he's one of those men who backs his words through his actions, and I consider him one of my brothers.

So on the morning when I most needed to hear his voice, he called. My cell phone was, as is often the case, somewhere mysterious. I could hear it ringing but couldn't locate it. When I punched in the message retrieve, I heard his voice. "Hey, Professor, just calling to check in and see how you're doing. You're probably in church preaching to the choir. Give me a call when you get a chance."

I called him back immediately and confessed that I was in a deep funk and needed to find some fishable water. Nothing more needed to be said. "I'll pack up and head out tomorrow. I'll see you in a couple of days."

When his ex-wife packed her things and moved from New York to the West Coast, taking their son with her, Tovatt folded up camp, packed his fly rods, and sold his Beaverkill home to fashion designer Tommy Hilfiger. He relocated to Grants Pass, Oregon, where he could be next to their son. He and his wife had met each other in an AA meeting and the union was not a good one. Again, water calmed. His new home sat above the Rogue River, where he could follow the migration of steelhead.

It takes Tovatt two days to drive from the Rogue to my home in Salt Lake City. When he arrived, we ate together with my family around our kitchen island. It's a comfortable and embracing space that invites stories and laughter. That night, there were plenty of both.

Early the following morning, we departed on a path that took us to one of Tovatt's guitar buddies, whose family owned a cabin outside of Lava Hot Springs. From the deck of the cabin we took in the sweet smell of sage and studied the broad sweep of land, unfolded before us like a quilt. Across the valley, an old John Deere sickle mower made slow loops around fertile hay fields in a hypnotic drone. And to our left, slipping down an aspen-lined ravine, a beautiful doe grazed on lusciously thick grass. Occasionally she would freeze, raise her head slowly, cock her ears, and listen for the unusual before returning to her feed. This landscape was deep balm for our souls.

We did the things one does in a small town. We stopped by the local fly shop, took a cup of coffee with the owner, picked up some flies, talked about the Portneuf, discussed the high river flows western states had been victim to, inquired about good access spots to the river, and, because of the ritual, were offered a couple of the owner's favorite places to fish. This came at the last minute along with a country map sketched on a piece of scrap paper.

Our first glimpse of the Portneuf confirmed what we'd already suspected: this small serpentine tributary of the Snake River was flooding over its banks. Access to stretches that looked decent were roaring tongues of mud and fanned out into coffee-colored flats. On several access points the water was impossible to enter, due in part to heavy brush. Perhaps, had we fished these stretches before, we might know how to enter the water, holding tight to the bank, feeling the solid ground underfoot. But stepping into unfamiliar water on such a runoff could be disastrous...even fatal.

Instead we continued upriver to a braided spot of the Portneuf, thick with cattails and bogged in mud. With some work, and careful not to lose our balance lest we fall over, we found solid footing and began working the river.

It was skinny water, surprisingly clear and shallow, but the casting was dreamy. I was above Tovatt and would look back periodically to see him casting to small rises. In the early evening light, golden against the vibrant slopes of green pastureland, the world suddenly righted itself—as it always does on the river. Occasionally I heard a howl when Tovatt missed a fish or, still better, a cackle when he hooked one. Soon I disappeared into my own rhythm, my Winston 3-weight, my favorite small rod, dry flies, and the occasional small trout as a bonus. Even though the trout were small, it took off the edge. I felt at peace.

Following a hearty dinner we sat on the cabin deck and marveled at the quiet. A young buck with fur-covered antlers nibbled sweet leaves, oblivious to us both. I crept off the deck and worked downwind of the buck, wondering how close I could get before being detected and before he bounced off and disappeared. Tovatt offered hand signals, and by taking short steps, staying hunched over and tight to the graveled road, and being protected by a slight cutback, I closed the distance. The buck saw me frozen in place and held me in his gaze without fear or concern. My legs began to spasm from the awkward posture. Finally, when he deemed I was of no significance, the buck bent his head and continued to eat again. I rose up, checked Tovatt's directions, and tried once more to close the gap.

At a point no more than fifteen feet away, I stopped and slowly stood upright. The buck rose up again and stared at me. His tail twittered, his ears alert, and I could see his face full on—deep, dark eyes directly locked in mine. He chewed slowly, stopping occasionally to mark me. I opened myself up and whispered to him softly, thanking him for this moment. I was both transformed and transfixed, astonished at how close I was allowed. Something unlocked inside me, and I felt the presence of everything holy and sacred in the natural world flood through me and into a larger universe.

I thought of my family: my daughter, pregnant with our first grandchild; my wife, Alana, who has been at my side for thirty-three years; and of my gentle son, John, who was getting ready to stretch out into the world in the artist's way. I thought of my brother, Barry, who disappeared many years ago into the deep mystery of Nicaragua, and of my sister, Sue, who has helped me in the most difficult moments of my life. And I thought of my friend Tovatt, standing watch, who knew instinctively when to appear in my life.

In this moment I was awakened again to the verity that my life has been a gift, and that all of it—behind me and in front of me—was and is on borrowed time. Knots unraveled in my shoulders, layer upon unhealthy layer, and I felt an emotional portal unlock. I was beginning to tear up when the buck suddenly startled and bounced off toward the road. I followed in his path, hoping not to lose the magic. It was exquisite.

Since the Portneuf River was a bust, we decided to fish Chesterfield Reservoir, a sixteen-hundred-acre body of water in southeastern Idaho, between Pocatello and Lava Hot Springs. Over the years, Chesterfield has quietly gained a reputation among fly fishermen for its large rainbow population. But Chesterfield, like the Portneuf River the day before, was unfishable. The wind howled across the reservoir, and whitecaps curled and marched across the water. It would be suicide to enter. Long in the face, we returned to the cabin, collected our kits, and took off for an afternoon at Lava Hot Springs.

That evening, after a relaxed day of floating in the hot springs, a massage that left us both drunkenly slothful, and a good dinner, we both agreed it was time to chase fish elsewhere. I called one of my dearest friends, the Captain, who lived only twenty minutes from Silver Creek, to see how the creek was fishing. The report for the Big Wood River echoed the common refrain of western waters: unfishable. Silver Creek, however, was fishing very well, so the following day we were off to hunt.

Two days on Silver Creek in float tubes catching big, angry browns on tiny, tiny flies cannot be adequately described. To say that it was unbelievable and the fish we caught were hot and game is hardly a measure at all. It's a very small part of the equation. What stays in one's memory is all the events and landscapes one travels before and after the moment. The hope of spring fly-fishing in a significant number of western waters had been brutally dashed by the tumultuous forces of nature. So to find ourselves in the great company of men we admired and respected, on a spring creek of great reputation, in weather that transfigured into chameleon land and light, was more than we could have hoped for. In the course of a single day we were exposed to whorls of light, powdery snow; dazzling rainbows of such color and clarity it looked as though they dipped into Silver Creek itself; and rumbling, brooding clouds— that shouldered atavistic myth—that were in themselves an offering of great benevolence.

Our drive back to Salt Lake was equal parts animated conversation related to the previous two days of fly-fishing and stretches of silence where each of us dissolved into our own private thoughts. Tovatt, I suspected, was thinking about his son, a wonderful young man who was functionally autistic and trying to work things out in a complicated world, and I, in turn, was thinking about a procedure—an upcoming surgery—that if successful might garner me two more years of quality life. But who really knows those things? It's a story I've heard before but the surgery had me concerned.

We'd just pulled out of Shoshone, headed south on a two-lane highway, when two large deer bounded across the road directly in front of us. They came so close and fast, fully stretched out in such blinding speed that I had only a fraction of a second to make a wheel correction to avoid hitting them. It was instinctual, without thought, and I split the space between deer, avoiding what we later realized would have been a horrendous accident. The highway beveled down a steep incline and we would most certainly have plummeted end over end in my Subaru Forester, or worse still, run head-on into oncoming traffic, a bloody mix of deer and metal.

When my head cleared and I settled down, I thought of all of it: of the capriciousness of life; of how one thing might lead to the next, or not; of how all things hang precariously on reflex and circumstance. I thought of how a second sooner or later might have altered our lives and the promise of life forever. It framed for me a sense of happenstance and chance. There are no guarantees in any of this, and what we believe we have in front of us cannot be played out with any certainty. Life was reduced to the simplest equation, and I could live with this. Whatever time I would be granted I would enjoy as I always had: in the company of my family and friends, all of whom have offered me love and light and laughter in the embrace of life.

THE STREAK

When Baltimore Orioles third baseman Cal Ripken voluntarily placed himself on the bench after sixteen years and 2,632 consecutive games, the longest streak in baseball's history ended. Baseball pundits were taken by surprise, fans were shocked, but Ripken knew what he was doing and so did I. The time was right.

I don't pretend to have anything else in common with Ripken other than a streak, but I understood him when he said, "There have been times during the streak when the emphasis was on the streak....It was time to move the focus back to the team."

For the past fifty years I have fly-fished the great trout waters of the West, enjoying all of it: days of heavy trout, days without a bump, evening sunsets with colors so rich in hue I could taste them on my tongue—every moment on the water a gift. But recently, I slipped. I made a mistake.

It wasn't intentional. I rendezvoused, as I have every year for the past umpteen years, in West Yellowstone with a group of fellow fly-fishing junkies. For more years than any of us can remember, we have come together every fall to wet a line, touch base with each other, fish, cook, drink fabulous wine, and stay in the loop of each other's lives. For all of us, this ritual, this journey, has become sacred. And because it has survived the other world—the world of failed marriages, hostile corporate takeovers, births, deaths, sickness, weddings, and the next generation—we guard it with great care.

We'd just finished working a stretch of the Firehole River and returned to Willie's cabin for dinner when the subject turned from food back to the topic of fishing. Several stories were recounted with great celebration, stories worth telling and retelling because we had all shared in them. Like Willie's afternoon on Buffalo Flats when he'd hooked into a beautiful plump trout and a pelican dropped out from the sky, trailed along behind the trout, snatched it out of the water, and disappeared back into the cerulean blue sky, taking Willie's line with him. We'd all seen the event—Willie holding his rod up in the air, not knowing quite what to do, the line whizzing into the backing before the tippet snapped. And when he came over to lunch and began to tell this exact story with great excitement and animation, we gave him "the look," like it was a bit early to be hitting the flask. It drove Willie crazy.

Or the night Charles Brooks, author of some of the greatest fly-fishing books regarding Montana water, wandered over to the cabin, already half in the bag, and joined us for dinner. Willie had invited a friend whom he thought Brooks might enjoy meeting. The man was a classically trained chef, a wonderful gentleman about Brooks's age, who had been in the Air Force during WWII and had flown "The Hump," just as Brooks claimed he had. It was supposed to be one of those great meetings, carefully orchestrated so that two people with similar stories could turn out to be lifelong friends. Instead, the evening turned into a nightmare and went downhill rapidly.

Brooks weaved wild stories soaked in whiskey and beer and played them out before the chef like a fat trout. Each tale got taller until the cabin was alive with the smell and taste of air battles, the intoxicating flavor of curried food from a crowded Indian bazaar, and the exotic perfumed scent of mysterious dark-skinned women smitten by Brooks's heroics.

Following each story, the chef declared that Brooks was full of shit. He challenged the authenticity of large and small details alike, and when Brooks didn't bite, the chef would storm off and fix himself another stiff drink, mumbling under his breath. But the chef wasn't a fisherman and Brooks was. For Brooks, the truth never stood in the way of a good story. We understood this about him because we understood this about ourselves. They were all fine stories.

On this particular evening, after we'd brought out and pumped life into our fishing stories, Wells asked me how many times I'd fished on the year. I'm fortunate to live close to one of the great trout rivers in the West, so I fly-fish a great number of days each year. And this particular year had been a banner year.

"One hundred and twenty-four days so far."

"You fishing slut!" Wells cried.

I could not deny that. It had been a particularly good year. Then Neubauer, an architect who journeys from the East Coast almost every year to join us on the river, asked a very simple question: "Been skunked yet?"

"Probably." To be honest though, I couldn't think of a single time that I'd been skunked. "All I have to do is look back across my journals to find out."

"You should do that, just to see if you have," he replied innocently enough. "That would be some kind of streak, wouldn't it?"

"But you know what happens to guys who get streaks going, don't you?" Wells asked.

I shook my head.

"They lose their hair. Think about it. Maris and Mantle. Remember? Maris's hair started falling out when he was chasing Mantle's record."

"Whatever," I replied, moving on to the next story.

But the seed had been planted just the same. That night, against my better judgment, I checked my journals.

At breakfast, before heading off to fish Coffee Pot, I walked over to Neubauer and said, "Not once."

"Not once, what?"

"I haven't been skunked yet."

"Seriously?"

"Seriously."

I don't know why I brought this up to Neubauer. It was under-handed. I floated the *streak* in front of him, and he picked it up and ran with it. He told the other guys, which left me in a position to feign off like it was no big deal, but still, it put me in the center of the claim... in the headlights.

Coffee Pot was a bust. The weather suddenly turned nasty—clouds darkening the sky; snow beginning to move downriver, quickly blanketing trees. We worked below the surface, running all the standard nymphs through our favorite runs. Nothing. Not a single bump between the five of us. Within the hour, with no signs of the snow letting up, we withdrew from the water and headed back to our rigs. Grabbing a plastic tarp to create a canopy over a park bench, we bundled up and tucked tight against each other and feasted on some of Wells's homemade deer sausage, several cheeses, duck pâté, and smoked salmon, washing it all down with four bottles of fat, rich wine. The weather was relentless. Wind picked up until the snow was horizontal, slashing around us in gusts, making any sort of fishing impossible. We packed it up and headed back.

Returning to the warmth of the cabin, we quickly shed our wet clothes, heaped up the fire, poured some stiff drinks, and watched the snow begin to enclose the cabin in a blanket of white.

Neubauer nudged me. "Too bad about the streak, huh?"

"The day isn't done," I said, leaving myself wide open for the challenge.

"You'd actually go out in this?"

I nodded my head.

"You're nuts! It's pounding down! The weather is insane and the roads aren't even navigable."

"You know what they say in Montana: 'If you don't like the weather around here, wait ten minutes and it'll change.'"

The words were prophetic. The weather got worse. To this day, I don't know why I didn't let sleeping dogs lie, but I was under the spell. Willie and Wells began banging pots and pans around the kitchen. It was their turn to cook dinner so I had some time on my hands. A smart man would have taken advantage of the evening to pour a healthy scotch, grab a good book, and do a bit of reading or catch up on conversations, maybe begin stacking poker chips for the evening's game. That's what a smart man would have done.

Instead, I announced to the boys I was going to head back toward Henry's Fork to a spot by Mac's Inn where I knew there might be a couple of trout holding against the bridge abutment. I'd be back before dinner.

Willie looked at me and said, "We'll be serving dinner in a couple of hours. Be careful." What he didn't say was revealed in his face. Had he said anything, it wouldn't have changed my mind.

Neubauer insisted on keeping me company. I didn't object. We slid out of the cabin, my jeep in four-wheel-drive, straining to keep on the small two-wheel path to the road. I assumed the highway would be plowed and salted. By the time we got onto the road, the plowed surface had begun to snow over again. This was just plain stupid but I couldn't turn back.

When we arrived at Mac's Inn, I left the heater running while Neubauer stayed in the warmth of the jeep. I quickly climbed into my waders, laced up my boots, tied a tungsten bead-headed zebra midge onto my tippet, and slid down the embankment and into the water. My second cast produced a plump little rainbow trout. I was off the hook. The streak was preserved.

I couldn't shake the disappointment I felt in myself for leaving the cabin to chase trout. My gesture was at best self-indulgent and at worst dangerous. Upon our return, Neubauer wove a fine story about us slipping and sliding along the road, me climbing out of my rig and nailing a trout without missing a beat. Drinks around and compliments on saving the *streak* fortified by a sumptuous dinner of elk steaks, nutted wild rice, and baby asparagus followed by a dessert of poached Anjou pears, several cheeses, and port wine created the illusion that I had accomplished something of measurable worth.

Deeper and more to the point, the *streak* began to own me. It was a narcotic. After that I began to fish harder, stay out longer, wade in spots I shouldn't have, take risks in sticky weather, develop superstitions, create rituals, and become edgy until I hooked a trout. I knew something had to give.

The 171st day of the streak put me in the company of the Captain, who owned a fly-fishing guide service out of Ketchum, Idaho. We rendezvoused outside of Jerome to float and fish a lake we knew was capable of producing several rainbow hogs big enough to tow a float tube and strip a line to the backing in the blink of an eye. We fished for twelve hours, catching and releasing more fish than I could remember in a long time. We had to pass the Silver Creek Conservancy on the way back to the Captain's house, so it just made sense we should drop in and fish a spot we referred to as the "Shark Tank."

We only fished the Shark Tank at night because that is when the big browns began cruising the water. It is complicated fishing for a number of reasons. Getting into the water is always a bit dodgy. There is no gradual way to enter into the slough. It goes from a slippery shallow to chest-high water in a few steps, and a false step can put you under in a split second. The water is cold, it is difficult to see where you are casting, so you are actually casting and setting the hook by your sense of touch. There are bats hunting the night for insects, and occasionally and unavoidably they latch onto a wooly bugger in the back cast. This can be very dangerous when practicing the principles of "catch and release." And once you hook into a huge brown, the odds of landing it successfully are complicated by the fact that these browns attempt, almost immediately, to wrap themselves around your legs and snap themselves off. But—and this is most certainly what draws us to this spot night after night—if you can dismiss all the reasons why one shouldn't fish in such water, the browns make it worthwhile. That night provided us both with some outstanding trout and a host of new stories. We arrived at the Captain's home around 2:00 a.m., snuck in a few hours of sleep, got up early, drank a couple of pots of coffee, filled up the thermoses, stopped at a convenience store for some smokes and whatever we could find to shove into our vests, and did it all over again.

There is no better fly-fishing than to be in the company of a great friend with no time constraints and nothing clogging up the universe. In those two days fishing with the Captain, watching pelicans fill the sky, the colors changing from liquid gold to shimmering purple, I never once concerned myself about the *streak*.

I left the following morning in a nasty windstorm and headed south toward my home. Gray clouds rumbled low across the sky, skulking like a scolded dog, and it began to rain heavily. At the cutoff to Silver Creek, I made a decision and turned my rig off the main highway and headed into the Nature Conservancy. I rolled across Kilpatrick Bridge, drove the long, narrow gravel road to the sign-in at the cabin, and stood under the roof and watched raindrops pummel the creek. From my vantage point I could not see a single person on the water. I was alone on the conservancy.

I trudged back to the car and slid into my waders and boots. I rigged up my fly rod and pulled on my Patagonia SST jacket. I selected a dry fly, ginked it, and slid into the water. I punched one single cast through the wind and watched as my fly passed untouched over the surface of the water. And then I began to laugh, imagining what this might look like to a pair of Silver Creek regulars. I could hear one or the other say, "I think I can smell a skunk coming on." They would laugh, staying warm inside their rig, knowing better than to fish in a storm like this and knowing without doubt that a dry fly of the sort I'd tied on would never touch the lips of any of these wily browns. "That old boy don't stand a snowball's chance in hell of catching a trout," one would say, and they would shake their heads.

And if they were there, they would never understand why a fly fisherman would make a single cast, retreat from the water, break down his fly rod, climb inside his rig, and simply drive off. What they would never know was just how "right" the moment was. Like Cal

Ripken, I was benching myself on purpose. I was ending the *streak* because it had become more important than the sport I loved. The pure childish bliss of fishing with the Captain, with nothing else in the world occupying my thoughts, was exactly the reason that I sought out water in my darkest moments. For the first time in a very long time, I remembered this and felt immediately humbled by the wildness of this landscape. I was home again.

THE LAST STEELHEAD

I am drawn to water. Rivers. Western rivers. And it is to the river I disappear when my life becomes complicated and confused. There have been many times when this has happened and always—always—the river has offered salvation. But the river is also a temptress. It seduces and teases and sings to me in a refrain that can disarm and make me drunk. In those moments a river can wound and kill. Twice in my life the Salmon River has taken me deep into its bosom, and on both occasions it has released me. It could have gone differently. More than twice in as many years this same river has saved my life. For me, the Salmon is a chameleon. It is a river of life and a river of death. In the most profound way, I am in its debt.

Thirty-six years ago, when I sought refuge from a failed marriage and set up camp on the banks of the Salmon River, it provided me an opportunity to disappear and rethink the direction of my life. If nothing else, filing that gold-mining claim allowed me to live on the land, read a whiskey-boxful of books, pan a little gold, and fly-fish all summer. At the time, it was deep balm for my soul. It was the first time I became invisible.

The first month of that summer I did little more than wander the banks of the Salmon, getting to know the curve of her body and the secrets of her trout. In the early-morning light, when the ice began to melt off the rain fly of my tent, I would build a campfire, drop a couple of eggs into a coffee pot to hard-boil for lunch, fish early in the morning, catch trout, pack them in my fishing creel, and later cook them over my old rusted box-spring grill.

During the heat of the afternoon, when the Idaho sun baked the landscape and the trout slid into the cool shadows of the river, I would seek shade in the pines, pull out whatever book I'd tucked into my fishing vest, and read. Sometimes I would eat a lunch of eggs, kippered snacks, and peppered beef jerky, and wash it down with a couple of long-necked bottles of cold beer. On other days, I'd throw my sleeping bag and pad into my rig and drive over Galena Summit, down through Ketchum and out to Silver Creek to fish for big brown and rainbow trout.

By midsummer I'd gotten to know a number of the local folks: the crazies, the ranchers, the cowboys, the river rats, the cattle barons, the bartenders, and the small-town cops. Often, after a long day of fly-fishing, I'd head downriver toward Sunbeam Dam to the natural hot springs, where I would submerge myself deep in the phosphorescent water of the Salmon. It was, in many ways, a purification ritual. At night, if the Braun Brothers were playing at Casanova Jack's or Harrah's Plywood Palace, I would head into town for a night of drinking and dancing. There was always a great crowd of people packed together on the dance floor, dancing buckle to buckle in the pulse and beat of the band. Those were hot nights, nights drenched in country music, whiskey, the smell of women, and the fine promise of sex. And on far too many mornings, I found myself in the dining room at the local Sawtooth Hotel, seeking a cure for my hangover, usually a good home-cooked meal by the owners, Steve (the Captain) and his wife, Kathy Cole. There was never a hangover bad enough that it couldn't be rectified by a thick stack of sourdough pancakes smeared in butter and drowned in maple syrup, a slab of home-cured ham, and a pot of heavy black coffee.

What surprised me about the years I spent, back to back, being nurtured by the Salmon River and protected by the arms of the Sawtooth Mountains, was this: I never formally met the Captain and his wife. It wasn't until fourteen years after first setting foot in the Sawtooth Hotel that I finally met Kathy by accident while on a fall fly-fishing trip with Kranes. We stopped at the hotel, as was our custom, for an early-morning breakfast before driving over Galena Pass to fish the Big Wood River. There was a small anteroom off the dining area that housed scenic postcards of the Sawtooth Mountains, handmade knives by Stanley local Al Sullivan, tapes and CDs by the Braun Brothers, sourdough starter kits, and book racks filled with paperbacks. After ordering breakfast, I wandered over to look at the books. Fully expecting to find propagandist literature warning against the reintroduction of wolves to the Stanley Basin area or Newt Gingrich's memoirs, I was astonished by the breadth and depth of the book selection. In this cozy little room was the work of some of the West's most lively writers. Jim Harrison, Tom McGuane, Barbara Kingsolver, Edward Abbey, Terry Tempest Williams, Bill Kittredge, Annick Smith, Pam Houston, Cormac McCarthy, David James Duncan, Norman Maclean, Nick Lyons, Wallace Stegner, and Louise Erdrich all shared equal billing. Kranes and I knew many of these writers personally and over the years had worked with many of them at various writing conferences throughout the West. It was simply dumbfounding to find such an array of seminal literary work in a town with a year-round population of fifty-nine people. I loved it. It offered me hope.

Two themes emerged from the literature: a deep concern about the western environment, and a passion for the open landscape and fly-fishing. When we asked our waitress who the curator of this little library was, she told us it was the cook. I felt I had to meet the cook in person to pass on my compliments, so I did something I would not normally do: I stepped into the kitchen, into its whirling blur of energy and motion. I found myself staring at a woman roughly my age. She was standing at the grill, frying bacon, eggs, slabs of ham, and sourdough pancakes while servers flew through the swinging doors carrying heavy plates of home-cooked vitals. Bussers scraped plates and crammed dishware into an old Hobart washer and cranked them through the wash cycle with lightning efficiency.

This was dangerous ground, entering a cook's kitchen without invitation, particularly during the busiest time of the morning. I didn't have time to regret it. I caught the cook's eye for a second, introduced myself, and quickly babbled out that I was completely astonished by her book selection. She stared at me, and in that stare I sensed the smallness of my preconceived notion that such books could only be found in big cities. It was an embarrassingly humble moment, one that I have never forgotten to this day. In an effort to make some sort of sense of what I'd said or, more honestly, to try to shift the conversation away from my blunderings, I asked her if she'd ever been to a writers' conference. She told me she hadn't but maybe that someday she would like to do as much. When I told her I had been involved in a writers' conference for "at-risk" high school students over the last six years, she simply stopped cooking and looked at me. She was sizing me up, trying to pull all these scrambled mutterings together.

"I'd surely like to do something like that for the kids up here," she said. "If you wanted to do something like that, you could even use the hotel during the slack season. Wouldn't that be cool?"

I went back and brought Kranes into the kitchen and made quick introductions. We started buttering toast on the line and she repeated the offer. "If the two of you want to organize a conference for June of next year, I'll let you use the hotel for free." On many levels, the offer was preposterous, beyond rationale.

"What exactly is your connection to the hotel?" I asked.

She burst out in laughter. "My husband and I own the goddamn place!"

We explained to her it might be difficult to organize something of this magnitude so quickly, but if she were indeed serious about the offer, we would do our very best to fill up a workshop. The following summer we began the Sawtooth Writers' Conference with our first session of ragtag "at-risk" high school students.

During our first summer conference, Kathy's husband, whom we had not yet met, approached us and asked if he could take us to the Kasino Club for a drink. There was something he wanted to talk to us about. That night, sitting in the bar waiting to meet the Captain, Kranes and I mused over the possibilities. All of them, unfortunately, drew a long list of negatives. We thought perhaps the energy of the kids, compounded by their outlandish dress, tongue piercings, and tattoos, was more than the Coles had bargained for.

The Captain sat down and got directly to the point. "I need to tell you this. Last year, when my wife told me she'd given the hotel away to a couple of writers she'd just met, who planned to run a writers' conference for high school students, I really had my doubts about her sanity." Kranes and I braced for the probable. "Don't get me wrong, I love my wife deeply but I didn't know what to think. I will tell you this and I mean it: this conference has changed our lives. It's made me look at kids who haven't had much of a life differently. So what I'm trying to say is thank you for letting us be part of this conference, and as long as Kathy and I own the hotel, you will always have a home here."

It was an emotional and heartfelt confession, so completely unexpected that Kranes and I didn't know what to say other than "Thank you for letting us be part of your lives." Until the conference ended, when the Coles gave their hotel to Albertson College some ten years later, they never balked on their commitment, even during some extremely stressful times.

When the Captain and I discovered our mutual addiction to fly-fishing, we became fast and furious partners in stalking trout in the great rivers and lakes of Idaho. We found it curious that in the earlier days, when I was living in the Stanley Basin, our paths had never crossed or not in such a way that we remembered each other. We have told stories of these early days: the reckless nights, the barroom brawls, the crazy misfits who hung to the edge of Stanley and disappeared into the landscape over and over again. In the telling and retelling of these stories, we discovered we'd often been in the exact same place at the exact same time. Because those were wild years, we've concluded that it was perhaps better that we did not know each other. Sometimes good fortune in friendship is simply a matter of timing.

Since my chance meeting with the Captain and Kathy, I have come to know their two extraordinary children and the Captain's father, Bob Cole, who was Bill Harrah's fishing and hunting guide on the Middle Fork of the Salmon River for over thirty years. Both the Captain and his father have schooled me in the ways of the steelhead and have taught me the history of the Salmon. It is a river dying a slow death; a river once teeming with salmon and steelhead, now being strangled by the monstrous hydroelectric dams of the Northwest. It is difficult now to reconcile the stories I have heard from old-timers with what I see during steelhead season. We make sloppy the value of the wild, and the toll has been exacted on this once great river.

I'VE BEEN EXPECTING the Captain's phone call, and when the phone rings late one evening, I know who it is without doubt. As always, when it comes to steelhead fishing, the Captain wastes no time.

"They're moving up. Not many, but they're here. Got any sick days coming?" he asks, priming the pump.

"Absolutely," I answer, getting up from the bed and taking the phone into the living room, where I won't disturb my wife. Already I'm feeling signs of flu coming on. "How's the temperature?"

"Not good. It's warming up too fast. Below Clayton it's muddy but from the East Fork up it's still clear . . . but I don't know how long that will last. I think this is the week you want to come up."

"Count me in. I've been packed since last year."

The Captain laughs because he knows it's true. It's a deep, conspiratorial laugh, one that signals an understanding between the two of us. The steelhead run, which begins in April, constantly puts us both at the ready. Compounded by the capricious nature of each year's weather, I need to be ready to depart at the drop of a phone call. So the arrival of the steelhead coincides exactly with an unusual strain of some exotic Asian flu I will contract. Because the window for steelhead fishing is completely dependent on the weather, I am packed by early February. If the temperature of the water is too cold, the steelhead move slowly and the run tends to be scattered and uneven. Conversely, if the temperature warms up too quickly, the snow pack will melt rapidly, carrying tons of muddy water into the Salmon River. This condition, referred to as a "blowout," turns the river into pea soup, making it impossible to sight-fish for steelhead. So whatever lie I concoct this time, it will be good. It's not that I do this often—in fact I'm never comfortable lying to my boss—but the steelhead are running, and time on the river is sacred to us both. There is a sense of urgency in the Captain's voice this season. There are other matters on his mind, and they are political.

This could be the last year for steelhead fishing in Idaho. In the backrooms of the National Marine Fishery, charts are being studied, numbers are being crunched, marine biologists are arguing about what specific designation should be placed on steelhead. They will either be placed on the threatened-species list, which might allow for sport fishing with a strict catch-and-release ordinance, or placed on the endangered-species list, which would forbid all fishing of them.

The thought cripples us so we will take no chances. In the early-morning light of the Sawtooth Mountains, in the numbing cold of the Salmon River, whose banks are swollen by an unusually high runoff, we will fly-fish for steelhead together. There will be little exchange of words between the two of us when we get on the water, and it suits our style well. We will fish close to fifty hours in four days. If we remember, we will probably eat, although there have been times when we haven't. We will leave the Captain's home in darkness and drive from Ketchum over snow-covered Galena Summit into the Sawtooth Basin. There will be plenty of dark, stiff coffee, maybe some doughnuts if we remember to stop and buy some, talk about steelhead, an occasional smoke, but little else.

There is a view from the top of Galena Summit out into the Sawtooth Basin which for the past twenty years has taken my breath away every time I break over the crest. I have never crossed into the basin without being touched deeply by the wildness of the country and bathed by the innumerable shades of the light and color of the Sawtooth Mountains.

The Captain is a second-generation fly-fishing guide, whose family roots are deeply embedded in the landscape of Idaho. To keep him out of trouble, his father used to haul him into the back country and put him to work riding fence line, working stock, and running pack mules into the hunting camps for Bill Harrah's high-rolling clients. It was back-breaking grunt work, and it honed the Captain to the land.

One summer, a sassy, no-nonsense cook showed up at the Middle Fork Lodge, where Bob Cole was the caretaker. The Captain fell in love with her and they married young. For several seasons they were the first into the lodge and the last ones out, closing up after the fall hunting season ended. Their nomadic lifestyle eventually took them back to Reno, where they both worked in Harrah's casino during the winter months.

The couple buried themselves in their work, pulling double shifts until they cached enough money for a down payment on a run-down hotel in Stanley, Idaho—population: 39. They were barely in their twenties. The odds were stacked against them but this was their dream.

Harrah took a liking to the "kids" and offered them some old cabins on a property he owned in Stanley. If the kids wanted them and could figure out a way to get them down to the back of the hotel, they could have them. So with help from some Stanley townspeople, they moved the cabins onto the hotel's property. That was over thirty years ago, and the cabins are still in place.

When their children were ready to enter high school, the Captain and Kathy moved over the summit into Ketchum, Idaho, where he became a captain for the Sun Valley Fire Department and took a second job with the Department of Highways, plowing snow to keep the treacherous Galena Pass open during the long winter months. The work is dangerous, and the Captain's truck has been buried in two avalanches. When this happens, he radios for help and waits in the frozen darkness of his reinforced cab until a crew arrives from Sun Valley or Stanley and digs him out. I like to believe that he passes the time by imagining himself fishing the brown drake hatch on Silver Creek or delicately casting #24 midges to picky trout on the Big Wood River.

There is a story the Captain told me once after a wonderful day of fishing together in the high Uinta Mountains of northern Utah. A friend of mine had loaned us his cabin in Christmas Meadows, and we spent the day fishing a small meandering stream that eventually empties into the Bear River. We fished with the most incredible fly rods, with reels no bigger than silver dollars—in a howling storm—and we managed to catch trout. At first we lost far more trout than we landed because it was almost impossible to set the hook. There simply wasn't enough rod to create the tension to hold on to the fish, who were spitting out flies on a regular basis. The wind never dipped below twenty miles an hour, and often we had to crawl along the brush-lined banks so we wouldn't spook the trout with our timid casts.

For the better part of the day I didn't see the Captain, although he was probably never more than thirty yards away from me. But I could hear him howling when he missed a set or hooting when he hooked a trout. Sometimes I'd just pop my head out of the reed-bordered banks, look downriver, and see an outstretched arm in a casting motion, making tight, clean loops in the wind. I'd watch as the line shot forward, the fly landing delicately on the surface of the water. When we came to the same conclusion—that the set was more effective if we stripped the line hard instead of trying to use the tip of the rod—our success ratio of landing trout doubled.

By early evening, windburned and giddy from a perfect day of fishing, the Captain and I headed back to the cabin to meet my wife and children. After regaling my family with our reenactments of the day's events, we stoked up the Monarch cooking stove, built a fire in the living room, threw some thick steaks on the barbecue, and took to a bottle of Talisker single-malt Scotch whisky. It was a perfect day.

Following dinner, and after an impromptu dance by my daughter and her best friend to the soundtrack of *Swing Kids,* the Captain and I settled back into the conversation of fishing. Because I was curious, I asked him if he'd ever had any unpleasant steelhead clients over the years.

"I've had a number of clients who don't really know how to cast, which makes it difficult to catch steelhead, but for the most part the people have been great."

It was the sort of answer I'd come to expect from the Captain. In the time I've known him, fished with him, drank with him, I honestly cannot recall him ever saying an unkind thing about a single person. Period. Unlike me, even in the heat of a good trout-fishing story he's never added on an extra inch to a trout or a pound to a big-lake trout, or exaggerated the number of fish caught in an afternoon. It's his only real fault, so I was surprised when he said he'd run into one real bastard a couple of years ago while guiding for steelhead.

A doctor from back East had booked the Captain for three days of guided steelhead fishing. He'd checked into the Sawtooth Hotel, where he'd also arranged to take his meals. The Captain has certain rules with his clients. He only takes fly fishermen, and he makes it very clear that if a client catches a steelhead, it must be released. Under current Idaho fishing regulations it is not necessary to release steelhead, but it had long ago become important to the Captain and his father that all their clientele should do so. Prospective clients who preferred to keep a steelhead were referred to other fishing guides in Stanley or Sun Valley. It was a sacred rule to the Captain, and he was extremely careful to make certain this was understood by fly fishermen who were interested in hiring him as a guide.

The doctor had the best fly rods and reels money could buy. According to the Captain, the doctor also had a splendid cast and knew how to play a big steelhead properly. By midmorning of the first day, the doctor had caught and released a number of small steelhead. Just before lunch, the Captain called the doctor's attention to the large steel-colored silhouette of a male moving up the river. The Captain instructed the doctor to be patient until the male slid alongside a female on spawning redd. When the Captain felt the male had settled down alongside the female, he instructed the doctor on the best way to cast to the steelhead, offered advice on measuring the line, suggested a trajectory for the cast, and personally tied on a fly he'd tied up early that morning. Within a half-dozen casts the water exploded, and the male burst out of the shallows and took to deeper water, stripping the doctor to his backing.

After a considerable time, with the male beginning to tire and getting close enough to the bank to land, the doctor made an announcement: "I'm taking this fucking steelhead home to mount!" he yelled over his shoulder. "Sorry about this, but it's legal and I want a trophy steelhead."

"We're going to release that steelhead," the Captain replied.

"I have no intention of doing that," the doctor pushed back, firm in his conviction. "I've got the right to take a steelhead from this river, and I plan to do so."

I asked the Captain what he said in reply, and he told me there wasn't a need—they'd both made themselves very clear about where they stood. So the Captain pulled out his knife, walked over to the doctor, and cut the line off at the reel. The steelhead dove down deep, the line trailing off and finally disappearing into the shadow darkness of the Salmon River.

The doctor threatened to sue, claimed that he'd bankrupt the Captain and his wife, file a grievance with Idaho Fish and Game, press criminal charges against the Captain for assault with a deadly weapon, or at the minimum, "I will own your fucking hotel and have your license revoked!"

In the end, none of this happened. The doctor broke his word but the Captain did not.

AS I WRITE this, the steelhead run is just beginning again, and I've thought a great deal about that story. My own migration to the wild water of the Salmon River began several months ago. I have dreamed about steelhead, lain with them at night underneath the northern stars, felt them shiver as they begin their treacherous migratory journey from the Pacific Ocean through Astoria, the Columbia River Gorge, up Bonneville Dam, the Dalles Dam, the McNary Dam, cutting east through the Lower Monumental Dam, Little Goose Dam, the Lower Granite Dam, and the Ice Harbor Dam, to the confluence of the Snake and Salmon Rivers, and finally to the waters of the Salmon itself. Like the Chinook and sockeye, whose populations of wild juveniles have decreased by 99% in only twenty years, the steelhead faces a slow death. Western states, strangled by an insatiable greed for power and by the politics and mismanagement of water, have seen the wild fish populations and habitats disappear almost completely. We have choked rivers with hydroelectric dams, logged fertile forests into mountains of slashed tree stumps, overgrazed livestock on river banks, torn out strip mines, dredged and polluted rivers—all without a shred of conscience or shame. We have divorced ourselves from the water and the water from ourselves.

In the course of a steelhead season, I will drive over two thousand miles in a ritual that returns me year after year to the frozen bank of the Salmon River. The drive goes deep into the reach of friendship and deeper yet, into life itself. I will cross over Galena

Summit and into the Stanley Basin, with the temperature gauge in my old rig registering well below zero. The first subtle curves of the river are as familiar and mysterious to me as my wife's naked body. Whispered in a chorus are the names of each bend: ZZ Top, Pontiac, Bridge over Troubled Water, Piece of Cake (where the river almost took my life once), and Suicide Rock, named for a miner— a spurned lover—who, in the dead of winter, leapt to his death and was swallowed into the darkness by the Salmon. The Fish Factory, Mother Fucker, the Pines, and the Death Wade all sing their own peculiar river songs.

In the river's memory is a story of a cold afternoon spent steelhead fishing with the Captain. We'd spent the day walking and driving the bank of the Salmon, hoping to get a glimpse of a steelhead. Perhaps maybe cast to one. It was a perfect steelhead day: bitter, bitter cold and all advantages in favor of the fish. Our hands and fingers were numb, so crippled by the temperature it made casting and reeling nearly impossible. And whenever either of us was in the river, the guides on each fly rod became frozen plugs of ice that had to be submerged in the river so a clean cast could ultimately be made. The reels burned ice-hot to the touch. Wind howled down the canyon walls in a haunting chorus that sliced across the Salmon, whipping it into frothy whitecaps. The light cut low across the beat of river we'd been working and provided perfect camouflage for the steelhead. The steelhead were in the water and we could feel them, tucked in, holding tight, but we could not see them. They had become invisible. There was an economy to our conversation. It was too cold to talk and our brains were numb. The idea of heading back to the cabin, where we'd build a roaring fire, drink a stiff glass of single malt, and consider the possibility of a hot tub, was hypnotic. But before doing that, before admitting to ourselves the day had been a bust, we decided to stop at one more spot: the Death Wade.

The Death Wade gets its name because of a powerful current that can sweep a steelhead fisherman off his feet in a careless split second.

Upriver from the Death Wade, the canyon walls have sloughed off into the Salmon, pinching and compressing the contours of the riverbank. There are many such dangerous runs like this on the Salmon during high water, but this stretch is particularly treacherous because the currents are powerful, the river rocks are slick, and there is no safety net against a fall. Also, there is no immediate slack water to recover if one should go under, no protruding rock structures one could grab at the last moment. If a fisherman goes under and his waders begin to fill with freezing water, it is all over. It doesn't take long for the body to completely shut down under such conditions. Such things have happened before on the Salmon River, and they will happen again. The danger is always present. In every moment and rush of water is the element of chance and risk. I am not fond of the Death Wade.

The facts are simple and it often feels like folly when we attempt a crossing to cast to steelhead. Yet we do. And because the river is so unpredictable and often difficult to cross, the pressure on the far side of the Death Wade is light and the fly-fishing traffic is often quite minimal. But the biggest draw is that there can be some monstrous B-run steelhead when the conditions are just right, and from across the canyon—where a rig can barely be pulled safely off the road—it is relatively easy to mark the dark torpedo silhouettes of fish. Secretly I was hoping we would not spot any steelhead. In all honesty, I was ready to tuck it in for the night.

Rounding a bend in the road, we could see that nobody was camped at the scrape of the shoulder we used to park our rig. It was encouraging on both fronts. First, there might not be any steelhead so our next stop would be the cabin with the promise of warmth. Second, there might be steelhead on the far side of the Death Wade and nobody had yet fished to them. We were chasing light but when we stepped out of the car and glanced across the Salmon, we could see steelhead. The light was absolutely perfect; clouds had opened up and we had a window. Nothing needed to be said. Quickly we pulled our kit together, dropped down to the river, locked our arms together, and pushed across the Death Wade for the first time. The current was powerful, and at least a half-dozen times either the Captain or I would do a gymnastic river dance, slipping and stubbing a boulder, and the other would tighten his grip and offer counterbalance. Almost halfway across the river the current slacked a bit, and we were able to let loose of each other's arms. We worked upriver until we were above where we'd seen the spawning steelhead and crossed to a bouldered bank. Slowly we climbed up a steep incline until we reached a deer path and then crawled along the path until we were at a vantage point directly above the steelhead. Carefully we peered down into the water, moving cautiously so we did not spook the fish. Then we saw them: two pairs of steelhead. The males, holding tight alongside the females, were thick backed with broad shoulders and the deepest coloration of dark blood and green.

The Captain whispered for me to double back the way we had just come, drop down into the water, and position myself way below the steelhead. I needed to be in such a position that I could watch the Captain's signals as to where to cast my fly. Once on the water, I could not see the fish because of the reflective glare off the river, so I depended on his instructions. My first cast was perfect, and when the steelhead fly swung across the nose of the male, the water exploded. The male had taken a swipe at the fly, panicked, and darted into the deep current. A single cast in a long and bitterly cold day and my turn was over. I retreated back to the ledge and relieved the Captain. He climbed into the water; I would spot for him as he had done for me. For the better part of an hour I offered small corrections to the Captain's cast while he attempted to catch the second steelhead. Finally, because the Captain did not want to frighten off the females, he withdrew from the river and crawled back to our overlook. The canyon wind had picked up again and the temperature was dropping rapidly. We pulled the hoods on our steelhead jackets tight around our faces and began a waiting game.

What happened next is beyond anything either of us had ever experienced on the river. As if by some calling—a curious instinct deeper than survival—both female steelhead left their redds and rose to the shimmering surface of the river. In perfect synchronization they porpoised out of the water and marked us in their eyes. That simple inconsistent motion exposed them to the real danger of predators, to eagles and hawks who wait patiently for just such a mistake. A miscalculation like this could make for a swift end. The Captain and I both understood this. Without conversation, we hooked our flies into the handle of our rods, nodded our respect to the steelhead, and slid down the scrabble bank and into the Salmon River. We locked arms and crossed the Death Wade for the last time that season. We'd been offered a gift, and we would honor it. It is in this water that I am constantly reminded that we are all on borrowed time.

THE WAY IT SHOULD BE

Straight out, in full disclosure, this is a story I wish were mine. I like everything about it, and if I could conjure up a way to pirate it, I'd do so in a heartbeat. But I'm suspicious when it comes to all things trout, particularly good trout stories, so this needs to come from the source.

Every fall, after a hectic summer working as a foreman for the Idaho Department of Roads, the Captain gets jonesing to slide out of the state and fish some new water. He and Kathy rent a fifth wheel and head off in whatever direction tickles their fancy. On this adventure, they made their way toward Craig, Colorado, so the Captain could fish the Missouri and Black Foot Rivers. Once they set up the rig at a campground, the Captain headed into town to visit a local fly shop. The campground, the Captain explained, was "full of trout bums," and at night the fly fishermen would congregate around a large fire pit, have some adult beverages, and talk about fly-fishing.

"So the next day I head into town. I stop at this fly shop and start looking around. I don't see anybody so I walked to the back of the shop and there is an older hippie guy with a gray ponytail bent over a fly-tying vise, tying flies like a madman. I started to say hello but before I could finish my sentence he turns around and yells, 'Dude, what the fuck are you doing here?'

"It caught me completely off guard," and the Captain busts up at this part, "he's fired up and yells, 'There's a blanket hatch going on right NOW! Grab some flies and get on the fuckin' river!' So I did, and had one of the greatest days of dry fly-fishing in a very long time."

I love that story on so many levels, and I make the Captain tell it every time our brothers in fly-fishing meet for our annual fall rendezvous. It's as fresh now as it was the first time I heard it. What else is truly required of any good fly-fishing story?

MARCH MADNESS

My friend Tovatt is older and wiser, and knows better than to take me seriously when we've had a banner day of fly-fishing based on a suggestion from the Captain that sounded preposterous—but wasn't.

This is how things happened: For years there have been whispers about a side channel of Magic Reservoir that is almost impossible to find and rumors about its large, pissed-off trout. Big ones. Phantoms. It's sort of like that childhood game *Telephone*, where someone whispers "I like cheese sandwiches" into the ear of the person next to them, and then it goes around the circle until it gets to the last person, who is supposed to then—with bated breath and excitement—reveal the original sentence but instead says, "I hate my father's new wife and I hope she dies and goes to hell." It's a showstopper at a birthday party, and it is soon disregarded once the utterer of the curse is sent home without party favors. But those who listened carefully know there is some truth in the utterance. So when the Captain brought the idea into the world to try and find this trout mecca, we were ripe.

Perhaps all trout Nirvanas begin in that fashion—a guide telling another guide or a fishing buddy about the secret that he's heard from a friend of a friend but it teeters on the implausible until somebody says, "Hell, what have we got to lose?" And off they go.

We've all been down this road before, chasing the dream of illusive trout. So much depends on the impulse of the moment and the luck of circumstance. In all probability, none of us on our own would have chased these phantom trout. But, perhaps because it sounded *just conceivable enough*, Tovatt and I left fairly good fishing on Silver Creek and headed for higher ground, literally.

I suspect what the Captain heard was something like this: Years ago trout began to move up the irrigation ditches when the water was turned off at Magic Reservoir. The ditches are nearly imperceptible to the eye, blending in seamlessly with the background of sage and rock. Add that to the simple fact that anybody heading for big browns on the reservoir would not be interested in an irrigation ditch that "might" hold trout. But somewhere along the line, perhaps at the end of a day of moderate to unsuccessful fishing, somebody looked at that scratch in the landscape and wondered about the myth and acted. Better yet, I can imagine this fly fisherman remaining for that *one last cast* after his buddies left him to his own devices. Finally, while heading back home to Ketchum, Idaho, having been unsuccessful at coaxing trout to the surface of the water, he made a decision that would forevermore change the way he looked at irrigation ditches. He turned back from the highway, followed the clawed, dusty two-track road up onto the ditch flat, and stepped out, only to see what clearly had to be something from another world rise to the surface to slurp a bug.

That night when he got home, his girlfriend angry at him for missing dinner at the Pioneer Saloon after promising he'd be home at a reasonable time, he could not find words for either apology or to describe the size of the trout he landed cast after cast. To try to explain what had happened would be to dilute this wonderful dream, and it would not be heard anyway after his inexcusable lack of manners. And although he knows he should have called or should have left with his buddies, sometimes these moments make for an impossible transaction. He will keep this secret away from his buddies and guard it like an infidelity that bears no good in telling to the world.

Then, in a moment of weakness, because it is almost impossible to keep such a secret for too long, he spills the beans, but not before securing an oath that his confidant will never, under any circumstance, in turn confide in another soul. Look, I understand this, and have been in such a pressure cooker myself. If you say nothing about a secret, how will anybody ever know how great the secret was? The logic behind this is something akin to the rhetorical question *If a tree falls in the forest and nobody is around, does it make a sound?* Similarly, if a man discovers a secret hole and doesn't share it with anybody, is it really a secret?

However, this secret found us in the flotsam and jetsam of life, and we decided to follow the whisper. After several dead ends, we stumbled onto something resembling a scratched-out road and followed it up to a flat where it paralleled the drainage ditch. So imagine this: four men in two rigs searching the Seven Cities of Gold, finally finding the map and exiting from their rigs only to see a shithole of an irrigation ditch, muddled gray with slate-colored water. There were some pretty long faces.

We walked the banks quietly as though we'd been swindled out of a dream. The water was low in many places, mid-ankle deep. Unimaginable water for trout. Carp perhaps, but not the noble brown trout. Most approachable access spots were protected by dense shoulder-to-shoulder foliage, making it impossible to descend into the water. And those few places where one could approach the water—if one was foolish enough to consider such madness—were so steep that getting out would be next to impossible. Did I mention brackish ooze and boot-sucking clay? It was not difficult to understand why no fly fishermen paid attention to this scar in the desert landscape. Seriously. Right?

I knew this dance well. Even under the worst foul-weather conditions, at the most unapproachable water holding little promise for trout, there are dance steps and a chorus required for the dance steps and the chorus that follows. Heads shake in disappointment, fly fishermen scuff their boots in the dirt, and the chorus of blame sits on each of their tongues.

Witness the scene, à la a Greek tragedy:

(Orchestral music at first, perhaps opera)

(Setting)

Four men dressed in waders, standing at the top of an earthen rise, looking first at the sweeping view of the Shoshone Valley. The audience hears nothing but the sound of the natural world—crickets, birds, and the screeching of hawks. Then the men turn and stare into the abyss. Slowly, a mumbling of sound, words, both recognizable and not until ...

"Do you think there are any trout in there?"

"It's awfully skinny water, isn't it?"

"No shit."

(Pause. Hope.)

"But there were trout under the bridge."

(Dashed hope.)

"But they were dinks."

(Rebuttal.)

"But they were trout."

(Trying the deeper biological.)

"To survive in this shithole these 'mythical' trout need to find deep holes."

(Sarcastic.)

"Like the ones in our fucking heads for coming here?"

(Light bulb moment. In chorus. Quizzical looks.)

"Let's see if we can find some deep holes."

"It makes sense."

(Smashed hope.)

"Even if there are trout in deep holes, how do you get down without tearing your waders and snagging up the line?"

(Said lightly [but with a tinge of real blame] and completely forgetting that every single person standing on the bank agreed to the campaign.)

"Whose idea was this?"

(The Finale)

Silence. The peacekeeper is about to speak when, on cue, a football-sized rainbow trout leaps from the murky depths of the aqua-clay water and the four men scramble to get into their waders, grab their fly rods, and find deep holes. And they catch BIG, FAT, ANGRY TROUT, larger than anything they could have imagined in this skinny water.

By the end of the day they will regroup, remove their waders, pull out flasks of scotch and whiskey, take deep pulls of these elixirs, clap each other on the back, recount each brown, and begin—although they know it to be a lie—to imagine they were the pioneers of this adventure.

The punch line, of course, is that they will all in turn reveal this secret at some point to a buddy after taking a sacred oath of secrecy.

If this makes any sense and if, dear reader, you have humored yourself so far with this diatribe, it might explain how, after the end of those five days of ridiculously sick fishing, a casual suggestion whispered into Mr. Tovatt's subconscious that he should purchase a camper so we could follow a fool's folly chasing trout all over the West would place us, some five months later, almost to the day, on top of a plateau in the middle of a horrific snowstorm, heading to the Green River with gale-force winds and the road disappearing under snow, with no option to retrace our path to safer ground and no place to go but down into a deep gorge, where we would chase the myth of winter-fed trout beginning to awaken to spring and eager for the fly. It's impossible to comprehend the depth of our depravity and disease.

We know the disease we have and we know, with equal certainty, there is no cure until one day we are forced to surrender and are returned to the sacred and the wild.

RIVER GUIDE

Brad Lovejoy is our river guide for two days on Utah's famed Green River, and he is the *real deal*. He is a throwback to the mythical West, a solitary man, deeply committed to Daggett County, Dutch John, and the Green River. He is both in the land and of the land.

Brad lives half the year in a fixed-up trailer on Guide Row at the end of North Boulevard in Dutch John, and guides the Green River for a top-rate fly shop in Salt Lake City, Utah, called Western Rivers Flyfisher. Like most seasonal guides he arrives in mid-March, opens up his trailer, double-checks all the particulars, and prepares for the onslaught of seasonal dudes. It's a taxing lifestyle for many reasons.

During the winter months our guide works for a contractor in Salt Lake City as a carpenter. "It's a great job," he says. "A lot of guides don't get good permanent work and so they're in debt when they show up. That's pretty tough on them." Brad is engaged the moment he arrives in the small Utah town. On any given day, when he is not on the water guiding, he is in all probability stalking fish, finding the spot nobody else has thought of before for his clients. It counts when a significant portion of your guiding income comes from being able to put clients on fish. "In the meantime, between guide trips you'd better figure out something to keep yourself occupied or it will get you. It can be a lonely lifestyle."

His boat is an old, battered first-generation ClackaCraft fiberglass drift boat purchased from the owner of the fly shop he represents. The original stickers are almost completely bleached from the sun. The inside of the cockpit is fashioned for a streamlined approach to servicing his clients with the least amount of energy expended. A selection of flies is readily at hand, sticking to foam pads superglued on either side of his seat. A cooler crammed with ice, water, Gatorade, and the day's lunch is within arm's reach so he can keep us hydrated in the scorching sun. Numerous stickers declaring his beliefs have been slapped onto strategic points inside the boat and read:

"Hunt hard, shoot straight, kill clean and make no apology."

"Kill your TV."

"Read a fucking book."

"Say No To Pebble Mine."

In a fashion, it is a cryptic composition that speaks clearly to a life he loves and lives.

Most anglers would be surprised to know how little a guide actually makes from a guided river trip. It varies of course, but a large percentage of the fee goes to the fly shop that makes the booking. Brad, like most guides, works as an independent contractor so there are no benefits, no retirement plans, and no medical coverage. Guides, if they are going to be lifers, need to find other ways to make ends meet. It's a spartan life by any measure, but it is honest and pure.

Lovejoy is inventive and has created work based on the needs of a largely farm-and-cattle community. During calving season he works in predator management. "I contract myself out to ranchers who hire me to call in coyotes. Basically they pay me a hundred and fifty dollars a day to keep their sheep safe." What this requires is a tremendous amount of patience, a vast knowledge of the patterns of coyotes, a steady hand, and the ability to pull the trigger when necessary. There is no room for sentimentality in this landscape.

"I used to get a good price for the skins, but the government now requires the hunter to cut heads off coyotes in order for us to collect a bounty. It is just stupid because the skin is of no use without the full cape." Before this requirement was in place, there were three streams of revenue to Brad's operation and he'd get paid every step of the way—for guarding the herd, from the government bounty, and then maybe a few extra dollars by selling the coyote's pelt. Severing even one of those lines of income was truly felt.

We floated the Green with Brad for two days. We selected a section of the river few clients ran because, although there were fewer trout, it was less crowded and the trout were larger. We liked the idea. For Tovatt and me both, it has long been that the fishing was what mattered and not necessarily the catching.

On our second morning, Brad apologized for his mood the night before when I'd called to invite him for dinner. "I had a tough night. When you called last night I wasn't all there. I apologize."

"Not at all, you were fine. Why?"

"One of the guides, a really good man, committed suicide yesterday while we were on the river. He hung himself."

On the other side of that confession all we could feel was the sorrow and the loss.

"I found him." There was a long pause. "We'd just had beers together four days ago."

"Did he say anything at all?"

"Nothing."

"It doesn't ever make any sense."

"He's like a lot of guides. He comes back from the winter deep in debt with the hope he'll get caught up. It must have just seemed too fucking impossible."

That night, Lovejoy and some of the guides got together, went out onto Flaming Gorge Reservoir, had drinks in crystal glasses, and toasted their friend. They told some stories, tried to make some sort of sense of it all, but in the end it is impossible.

The wild is not a landscape of *maybes. Maybe we could have seen it coming. Maybe if he'd just said something. Maybe we just didn't see the clues.* If the river is truly part of you, if you are in it at its best and worst, with all the distractions and seductions, you know full well how every day in the wild is a lesson in survival. And if you forget, if you are misled by her calling, sometimes she can whisper to you in such a voice that you believe in the folds of her darkness. And what she whispers is this: *Beware, young dreamer, beware. If you are a tormented soul you do not belong on my river.*

When reality and the dream world collide, the collision is harsh and brutal. That night I heard the howl of a coyote, perhaps the one I saw limping on the plateau with a mangled paw. My good friend snores in his berth at the front of the trailer. Cancer eats at my bones. A guide's mother hangs her head down and cries, and trout hold close to the bank in the pale moonlight.

NO NONSENSE

I first met Bob Cole on the bank of the Middle Fork of the Salmon River. At the time, he managed the Middle Fork Lodge for Bill Harrah. In the world of backcountry fishing and hunting, Bob was a legend as a guide. The lodge itself was used exclusively for Harrah's high rollers, and it was Bob's job to make certain he provided the big spenders with whatever it was they wanted. Everything—the booze, food, hunting and fishing equipment, and accommodations—was *top drawer*.

The Middle Fork Lodge is located in the rugged landscape of northeast Idaho, about ninety miles northeast of Boise, Idaho, and sits almost dead center in the state. It is part of the Frank Church–River of No Return Wilderness Area, and there are only two ways in or out: charter flights or rafts.

My first conversation with Bob, as I recall all these years later, was brief. Alana and I had been invited on a float trip down the Middle Fork by restaurateur Pug Ostling and his wife, Carolyn. Their son and my godson, Morgan, was working at the lodge so we thought we'd pull off the river and run up and say hello to him. Morgan was somewhere on the ranch, but Bob made no effort to go get him. I liked Bob immediately. Work was work. There was a moment of awkward silence.

Finally Pug said, "Metcalf is a fly fisherman. He fishes a lot."

"Is that so?"

"Yes, I do."

And that was the end of it. No follow-up of polite conversation. We put back on the river and I couldn't help sensing that somehow our paths would cross again. It seemed, at the moment, a rather preposterous notion.

It would be nearly twenty years after my first encounter with Bob before I would meet him again, at a reading by the students and faculty of the Sawtooth Writers' Conference. The reading was to thank the townspeople of Stanley for being so gracious to us. When it came to the faculty portion of the reading, I read a piece that had recently been published in *Drake* magazine called "The Last Steelhead," about fly-fishing for steelhead with the Captain. (It later became a chapbook published by Elik Press.) It was a lamentation for the once wild waters of the Salmon River, a requiem of sorts for western waters with decimated fish populations from river damming.

Bob was sitting up front with his wife, Virginia, and twice during the reading I heard him sniffle. When the crowd died down I went over to re-introduce myself.

"Mr. Cole, I'm Jeff Metcalf."

"I've heard about you."

"We met many years ago on the Middle Fork, at the lodge."

"I don't remember."

"Your son and I fish a great deal together."

"He's told me."

"Do you still fish?"

"Some."

"Steelhead?"

"Yes."

"Well," I said, working unsuccessfully to draw out a full sentence, "maybe I'll see you on the Salmon this April."

"Probably."

"Nice meeting and visiting with you both," I offered awkwardly and then began to walk away.

Over my shoulder I heard Bob say something. I turned back.

"It was a real good story," he said quietly. "Real good."

"Thank you."

That April I headed north toward Stanley for steelhead fishing with the Captain. On the days he wasn't guiding we would fish until it was beyond dark. Bob and Steve, father and son, owned the Sawtooth Guide Service for thirty years. Bob had personally given up guiding many years before but his love for steelhead never waned. The three of us would fly-fish together, and when Bob got to talking about the old days of salmon, steelhead, and redfish runs I listened like a small child because he had been there and so, as a child, had his son. Bob carried the memory of these fish in his bones. Deep pools of salmon on the Middle Fork, where *dudes* could not help but catch salmon and then—as so much of it is always with men— the bragging rights of those *dudes* around the camp cocktail hour.

"Even a blind man couldn't help but hook a salmon," he'd say, laughing. And then, in the pause, I could see the rest of the story in his face: the gradual disappearance of the wild from the wild. If a person did not know the history of these rivers they might easily dismiss Bob as an old man reminiscing about the good old days that never existed. But those days *did* exist; they are recorded in the photographs that reside in the Sawtooth Historical Society and in the narratives of men who fished the runs.

I hold this image of Bob Cole in my head: It was midday and the sun was out although the temperature was still only in the mid-twenties. We'd lunched up pretty well that day because Bill Selvage, our mutual friend, was in charge of the menu. To this day, I don't know whether to curse Selvage or sing him high praise. When he became part of the annual steelhead fishing campaign he always made us stop for lunch—gourmand lunches that even on days of the foulest imaginable weather would often transport us into another world. On this day, the lunch was exquisite. Bob suggested we take a gander at Torrey's boat ramp to see what was going on. He'd seen some steelhead holding in the water earlier in the week and thought it might be a good idea.

The boat ramp itself provides an easy and gradual approach to the Salmon River. There was a rig pulled into the spot Bob had thought about fishing. We parked a fair distance from a couple of out-of-state fly fishermen. For about fifteen minutes the two men messed about with their waders and flies, talking about what weight rods they should use, until finally Bob got out of his truck and simply said, "I'm going to go catch me a steelhead." He reached into the back of the bed to retrieve his fly rod, and headed down to the river. He walked directly past the two fishermen. By their change in posture it was clear that they were surprised some "old guy" would walk out in front of where they were clearly going to fish. Compound the scene with this visual: Bob didn't wear fancy breathable waders and sport a Patagonia or Simms vest filled with a thousand steelhead flies. He wore a pair of neoprene boot waders that had been cut off just above the knees and used a pool cue as a wading staff. Suspenders held up his Levi's, and he wore a wool Elmer Fudd hat tilted at an angle to block out the sun. After about two-dozen casts, Bob hooked and landed a beautiful steelhead. Then he released the steelhead back into the water and walked back by the two fishermen, who still weren't completely geared up.

"Hey," one of the men said, "we were going to fish there."

"Go ahead," Bob replied. "I'm done."

And that was it for Bob. It was just that simple. Some people fish and some people talk about fishing. Bob didn't have time for the latter.

As I write this memory of Bob, I am laughing out loud. I am halfway around the world, in a small cafe in Verona, Italy. I'm having an espresso coffee. I'm looking out onto Lake Garda to a pier where a number of anglers are casting off a dock. An old man walks to the end of the dock and plunks himself down between two middle-aged men. He puts something magical on his hook and makes an impressive cast into the water. Moments later he is reeling something in and the other men look annoyed. It could be a perch—some form of shad, maybe even a northern pike. Who knows? Then he puts the fish in a five-gallon bucket, picks up his collapsible chair, and walks off.

I can imagine one of the men saying, "Hey, we were going to fish there!" And I can only imagine the reply from the old man: "Some people fish and some people talk about fishing."

FISH FINDERS

We didn't say anything the first day of fly-fishing on the Madison River, but we all noticed. Every single one of our ragtag fall fly-fishing group was paying attention. It was, after all, a rare sight. Biggs, that is, catching the first, the most, and the biggest of the gnarly browns and rainbows. It's not that we counted trout, or if we did, we did it quietly and privately. For most of us that need to count trout had long ago lost its importance. But this was so remarkably queer we couldn't help but notice, and we began to wonder about Biggs's good fortune. Indeed, it was as if he had been anointed by the fish gods on this first day of our trip. There could be no other explanation. We'd see about the next couple of days.

Every October a group of us would meet in Ennis, Montana, to eat, drink, play cards, fight with each other, and fly-fish together. Most of us had known each other in college or been together in fraternities or grew up with each other. This story is framed in the early '70s, when the country was recovering from an ugly part of our history: a foolish war, student riots, corrupt politicians, and an incalculable and senseless loss of life on both sides of the ocean. Our group included combat veterans, a conscientious objector, a lawyer, a fighter pilot, a couple of pilots who flew cargo in and out of Vietnam, an architect, an engineer, and a computer whiz kid who was inventing simulators before we all knew what computers were. Whatever our body politic was, it was understood by all that it stayed outside the river. We were here to reach out to each other, to stay in the loop and try to keep connected for as long as we possibly could before life swallowed us up into our own worlds.

Biggs had probably fly-fished less than any of us in the group, and his good nature and sly, understated sense of humor made him one of the most pleasant men to be around. Often, at the end of the day, at the beginning of the cocktail hour, when we recounted the strikes, the trout we'd stuck and lost, the trout that came unbuttoned, and offered our thoughts on what the hot flies might be, Biggs would simply listen, taking it all in and enjoying the good providence of circumstance. On this particular night, after the banner day we'd witnessed, Biggs offered no more than his usual sly nothingness. This drove us crazy, and we all wanted to know what the secret fly was, but to ask was an admission of failure. Besides, it was only the first day on the river and we still had three more days to go. Tomorrow would be different; we'd all wait and see. Biggs would be back to his old hit-and-miss. The template would fall back into place, and the world as we had come to know it would be realigned. But that didn't happen. The next day Biggs buried all of us, and more than a few of the men were starting to get annoyed. "Pissed off" would be a more accurate description.

That night, sitting outside on the deck drinking cocktails, Nuts broke the silence and asked Biggs what the hell was going on. Had he, in fact, taken some advanced degree in angling? He was driving us insane. That, Biggs swore, wasn't the case. In fact, he himself was a bit surprised at his good fortune.

"I don't know. I'd forgotten my sunglasses and when we were getting our licenses at the tackle shop, I bought a pair of 'fish finder' sunglasses."

"Fish finders? What are you talking about?"

"The owner showed me these glasses. They're the new thing in eyewear. Polarized glasses. He guaranteed I'd be able to see the trout better than anybody else."

"And you bought them?"

"It's the latest. The polarized lens helps break through the glare. He had this cardboard cutout the manufacturer sent with the glasses.

It said, *Want to see more fish? Try these on!* It just looked like a piece of cardboard but when I put the glasses on I could see a bunch of fish, so I bought a pair."

"And?" Nuts asked.

"And I can see trout. You guys don't own them?"

It silenced all of us and I could begin to see everybody scheming. I knew for a fact that at first light I would be at the tackle shop to get myself a pair of fish finders. Judging by the conspiratorial glances on the deck, I wouldn't be the only one.

By the time I rolled out of bed, pulled my kit together, and made my way down to the tackle shop, the boys were already standing over by the counter where the glasses were prominently displayed. They all had fish finders on and were looking at the cardboard cutout of trout and mumbling approval and astonishment. It looked like a blind fly-fishermen's convention. When the owner sauntered over and asked if he could help us out, Nuts spoke up for all of us.

"So, how much for fish finders?"

"A hundred and twenty-five dollars for the day," he replied, straight-faced.

"For fish finders?" Nuts asked incredulously. We all began to take off the glasses slowly and put them back on the rack when the owner added, "Only around here. We call them fishing guides." Then he let out a laugh that let us all know we'd been gooned. "Get it? That's what guides do... they find fish." I couldn't help but wonder how long he'd been waiting for some city boys to come in and ask the question. We all busted up and we all purchased fish finders.

That afternoon, spread out around Varney Bridge and working the fingered side channels of the Madison, we must have looked like escapees from *The Blues Brothers*. We were smiling and laughing as we stuck fish for the first time in a couple of days. It was, by all measures, an unparalleled day on the river.

In many ways we've lost touch with each other over the years. It just happens when life catches up with you. But I will say this:

whenever I'm rummaging through one of my fly-fishing bags looking for a box of elusive #24 midges, and I find those old fish finders busted up and broken, it returns me to the Madison, to when all things in the universe were in balance.

ONE EYE

Willie and I bid on two days of steelhead fishing on the Salmon with our good friend the Captain through a fundraiser for the Sawtooth Writers' Conference. On the first day of our fishing trip, stalking steelhead along the banks of the river, the Captain asked us for a favor.

"Any chance I could get you to fish with my new partner, Dean? I want to get your take on how he guides."

We were happy to accommodate him since we'd all be fishing together on the days when he wasn't guiding. That night, Willie and I discussed the Captain's decision to sell part of his company to an outsider. Bob Cole had long since retired, so it made sense that the Captain needed help during steelhead season.

The following morning, we waited at McCoy's Fish and Tackle shop on Ace of Diamonds Street in Stanley, Idaho. Dean was about twenty-five minutes late, which is a cardinal sin as a guide. At six hundred dollars per day, it's bad form to keep your clients waiting. But Willie and I are both pretty easygoing when it comes to fishing. We've fished side by side for over thirty-five years, and although our trips are about fishing, these adventures are as much about getting together and keeping in touch as anything else.

After Dean slid into the parking space next to ours, he apologized for being late and then asked us if we brought lunch for him because he hadn't had breakfast and was hungry. Willie looked at me and I gave a slight nod of my head. Strike two.

Making our way downriver, stopping periodically to look at some of the most likely spots to headhunt steelhead, Dean made a disparaging and racist comment about Asian Americans. It shocked us, and we both bristled. Willie's wife is Asian American, and I could feel him starting to come unbuttoned. I reached over and touched his leg. His body tensed. In all the years I've known him I've only seen Willie lose his temper a couple of times, and it wasn't pretty. I sensed he was about to say something when we spotted the Captain fishing with a couple of our good friends, Terry and Hans Carstensen, who have generously contributed their Crooked Creek property every year for our steelhead fishing excursions. We pulled over.

The Captain came out of the water to talk with Dean. Willie and I wandered up to see if the steelhead were moving upriver. The day before had been slow, the temperature barely breaking freezing, and the steelhead were slow. When we rejoined the two of them, they were discussing how they would leapfrog over certain favorite spots, splitting them equally, sharing the river. When the Captain asked how things were going I simply replied, "Interesting." We'd talk later on.

Dean contributed very little to the morning. Often, when he studied the water and proclaimed there weren't any steelhead, Willie or I would point to some on redds in places the Captain had taught us to look. Just before lunch, Dean put us both on a steelhead at Suicide Rock. Willie waded across the river and fished to the steelhead, making conservatively over a hundred casts while Dean and I spotted for him. Finally, Willie waved me down to step in and see if I couldn't interest the fish in a few of my flies. After about a half hour, I withdrew from the water and the three of us sat down for lunch. We listened as Dean talked about himself.

Lunch, as always with Willie, was a veritable epicurean feast. Good wine, rich duck pâté, a myriad of cold cuts and smoked sausage, good Bigwood sourdough bread, and birdseed cookies, all followed up with rich dark chocolate and red wine. As we ate, Dean announced he was going to fish for the steelhead neither of us could touch. Jokingly we told him to knock himself out, and he grabbed his fly rod and took off. We didn't follow him but began a serious discussion about how we would talk with the Captain. It occurred to us that perhaps in some way the Captain regretted his decision to partner up with Dean, and he wanted an honest appraisal of his new partner.

Dean returned, never having touched the steelhead, and—while polishing off the last of the cookies—suggested that we should move downriver. Something bothered me about this. I told him we weren't done eating and we'd let him know when we were ready.

"In fact," I said, "during lunch while you were fishing, I realized why we didn't touch that steelhead."

"Why's that?"

"We were watching you cast, and I noticed the steelhead was blind in one eye." It was a complete lie because Willie and I hadn't moved during lunch and had, at this point, no interest in Dean and, furthermore, no need for his lack of guiding expertise.

"Bullshit."

"You'll see."

I grabbed my own fly rod and went out into the water. Part of me did it because I felt bad I hadn't called Dean out on several occasions during the day but also because he was the opposite of everything a good guide should be. Dean waded out with me and stood off to the side, telling me where he thought I should cast.

"You're casting on the wrong side," he barked.

"Don't tell me where to cast!" I yelled back. "What you don't understand is that this steelhead has a bad eye so the cast has to be on the other side of him." Before I could tell him to go fuck himself, the water exploded and the steelhead ripped through the water. In a matter of a few minutes, Dean netted the steelhead. As he bent to remove the fly he stopped and looked over at me.

"It's missing an eye," he said.

"Yes," I replied.

"I'll be go to hell," he said quietly. "You could actually see he was blind?"

"Yes." It was an absolute lie.

Willie and I had already decided we were done with our guide; we'd go hit one more spot and bid farewell to Dean. The most difficult part of the experience was yet to come: how to talk with the Captain about his partner when we gathered together for dinner? For both of us, the Captain is family. Nobody likes to hear that they've made a mistake in judgment. Our feeling was that Dean offered nothing to one of the most respected guide services, and that his day with us reflected none of the values the Captain had built his reputation around. We decided we'd let the Captain ask the questions and we would answer them honestly. As it turned out, matters took care of themselves.

Dean suggested we hit a spot called the Fish Factory. It's a terrific stretch of the Salmon River with an off-road, boulder-strewn dirt scratch of a trail that parallels the river. If the water is at the proper depth the steelhead find ideal situations for spawning. There are, as always, some drawbacks for fly fishermen. Spotting steelhead at the Fish Factory is almost impossible because of the constant glare from the river, and the road into the spot is barely wide enough for a single rig, so meeting another rig coming in the opposite direction can become a real pissing contest.

More problematic for the spotter and fisherman is there is little cover to hide and study the river, and it's easy to spook the fish. Any suspicious movement on the bank and they scatter quickly. Once a steelhead is spotted from the road, the fisherman has to navigate steep terrain down to the river on razor-sharp rock shards that slide underfoot to get into position to make a cast. It's slow and sketchy. One misstep can easily set off a slide, resulting in the fisherman ending up in torn waders at the water's edge. Over the years we've all had our fair share of misfortune.

Once in the water, the canyon narrows slightly so the water pushes hard, and one has to cast midway across the run toward the bank where the steelhead most often hold. It's almost impossible to see where the steelhead are without somebody spotting overhead and yelling instructions on extending or shortening a cast, mending quicker, or leaving the fly in the water longer on the swing.

Willie and I took turns casting, and we each caught and released several healthy and hot A-run steelhead. Across the river we heard the honking of the Captain's rig and watched as the Captain jumped out and ran down to the water's edge, where he hollered across the river for Dean to come to the bank. Dean waded across the river and soon Willie and I decided to follow suit. Judging by the Captain's animated body language, we were certain he'd found a great new spot for steelhead and wanted to let us know about it. Despite how our day had developed with Dean, it would be a pleasant diversion to cross the river and visit with the Captain and his clients. The Carstensens had flown out to Stanley for a week of steelhead fishing with the Captain, and we hadn't seen them since the previous season. We hoped they might be available for dinner.

I've only seen the Captain angry a couple of times in my life, and as we got closer it was clear this wasn't a stop to relay steelhead information. He was visibly upset, and we could hear him dressing down Dean.

"Didn't I tell you to leave the Fish Factory for us?"

Dean was backpedaling and offered a weak excuse to the Captain. "We thought you'd already fished here, so we thought we'd see what was going on," he said sheepishly.

There was no mistake about what had transpired. Willie and I knew that Dean had intentionally disregarded the Captain's earlier directions. We'd been downriver all day and there was no possible way that Dean had misunderstood the Captain. And there was no way that the Captain would have passed us along the way without a honk from his rig to let us know where they were. We had not been privy to the earlier discussion of who would fish certain beats along the Salmon. Had we known, we would not have disregarded the Captain's request. It would be one thing to come upon a stretch of water and find some other fly fishermen working the Fish Factory. It happens all the time. But for his own partner to intentionally try to steal the run was simply inexcusable.

I thought of something the Captain had said to me one late evening on Silver Creek: "The measure of a man is not how he fishes, but how he governs himself on the water."

I thought of this as Willie and I made our way over to apologize for not asking what stretches he and Dean had worked out the previous night. Clearly the Captain was embarrassed about his outburst and having us witness it. Immediately we offered to head downriver and look for another spot, but the Captain wouldn't hear of it. He knew we would never do such a thing and it troubled him that his partner would do so without hesitation. He wanted to move downriver himself and put things right. Given the day so far, it was probably the best thing to do. We'd meet up with the Captain and the Carstensens later on that night for dinner. Dean would not be invited.

When the Captain drove off, Dean came over and suggested we stay put since there were plenty of steelhead holding in the run. He made a brief comment that there had been a misunderstanding between the two of them and everything would work itself out. Without even the briefest of conversations between the two of us, Willie told Dean that we were done with him for the day.

"Because of this?" he asked incredulously.

"Yeah, that was fucked up, Dean. Really fucked."

"We're going to take you back to McCoy's, Dean."

"But you paid for a full day."

"Not with you. We're finished with you."

That night at dinner, before the Carstensens arrived, the Captain started to apologize for his behavior. We cut him off. There was no need to apologize for anything. In the end, it was not necessary for the Captain to hear our appraisal of his new partner; Dean's actions spoke loud and clear for themselves.

The Captain ended up buying out Dean and eventually selling the Sawtooth Guide Service to a wonderful woman, Julie Meissner, who continued to run it in a manner that reflected the Captain's own deep commitment to the Salmon River and to those who had the good fortune to ever be on the river with him.

RIVER JUSTICE

Rising high above the Salmon River, just below Sunbeam Dam, is an outcropping of jagged rock considered by many spin fishermen to be the best spot to catch steelhead in their migratory pattern as they move upriver to their spawning grounds and finally to the Sawtooth Fish Hatchery.

The water beneath the dam is violent, exploding like molten lava at the touch of water. The press of water is compressed and funneled through a narrow gap where the dam had been breached some twenty-four years after its construction and twenty-three years after it ceased to be useful to mining interests.

For old-timers of Stanley, Clayton, Challis, and points both up- and downriver of Sunbeam, it is a bitter reminder of what the river once was and how the damming of Idaho rivers created impenetrable barriers for migrating steelhead and sockeye salmon. It is a sad and cautionary tale repeated over and over in the landscape of the West.

During steelhead season, in the early-morning light, as we make our way slowly down the Salmon River looking for steelhead, we play a sort of game—placing bets on how many rigs will be lined along the road and how many metal slingers will be balanced precariously atop the cliffs waiting to snag a steelhead.

The first time one sees this spectacle of perhaps twenty to thirty men, fishing poles in hand, dressed in foul-weather gear, braced against the cold and staring into the deeps of the Salmon, the most obvious question is hardly ever asked. It wasn't until the third or fourth time we'd driven past the dam that I finally asked the Captain how they kept from tangling up on every cast.

"They don't all cast at once. It's based on a rotation system."

"Okay," I replied, like I often do when I'm not exactly awake and firing on all cylinders.

"One guy casts, and when he hooks into a steelhead he moves down the cliffs to a spot where he can beach the fish. A lot of times the guys at the bottom help him out. Then the next guy steps in his place and casts. It's pretty slick and everybody understands the rules."

"Everybody?"

"Most people, or they don't last long."

"Meaning?"

"It don't work out for them if they don't get it."

Then the Captain told me a story about this dude from back East that had a very difficult time grasping the protocol. After he muscled his way up the cliff and attempted to bully his way to the top of the casting chain, a couple of the old boys lost interest in his shenanigans and asked him what he thought he was doing. He explained that he'd been steelhead fishing and hadn't landed a single fish. When he said he had to get a fish before he left town and he didn't have time to wait in line, one of the fishermen grabbed his pole out of his hand and threw it down into the river. "There you go. You can fish all you want now."

Although the next part of the story can't and would never be confirmed by anybody on the cliffs, the man either tripped or was helped over the side and plunged into the river, only to be spit out of the water several hundred yards from where he crashed into the rapids.

I don't doubt the story—once or twice every season some angler goes for a swim, either of his own volition or with the assistance of another angler. In this wild landscape, these governances are understood and are sacred. To violate the order of things is potentially dangerous business, and I can respect the vigilante nature of the solution.

DICK CHENEY, DICK

We got the phone call early evening. The then vice president of the United States, Dick Cheney, would be fishing the South Fork of the Snake River. Again. And we all knew what that meant. There would be a clusterfuck of Secret Service and FBI agents driving shiny black suburban SUVs and Hummers with tinted windshields and bullet-proof windows at breakneck speed through the small town of Irwin, Idaho, headed toward one of the boat ramps. Prior to Cheney's appearance, Black Hawk helicopters had been observed making several sweeps of the river's canyon ridges, looking for potential threats to the vice president's life. "There will be all sorts of eyes in the tree line looking out for Cheney," one of the guides said, and I did not doubt him.

A team of Navy SEALs would be in the water at all times. A fair distance from the vice president's drift boat there would be high-speed zodiacs with secret agents and special forces at the ready, armed with enough automatic weaponry to take over a third-world country. At first, Cheney's fly-fishing trips on the Snake River were a novelty. You know, small town and all. But after many such visits in an unreasonably short time, the celebrity of his appearances began to lose its magic. The residents' unspoken resentment had nothing to do with politics at all—Idaho had only voted Democratic once since 1964; this red state loved President George Bush and Vice President Cheney. It did, however, have a great deal to do with river protocol.

The Snake River is widely used for a variety of recreational activities. Power boaters, kayakers, drift boaters, canoers, and rafters—diverse communities that are, in many parts of the country, often at each other's throats—have struck a remarkable balance. Part of the success of this marriage is due to the landscape of the Snake. It is a wide-open river with a number of side channels to explore, convenient put-ins and take-outs with small islands along the way to hold up and fish or take a lunch break. It also works because the rules don't change. It doesn't matter what sort of river craft a person fancies, if you're going to put in at one of the many boat ramps, you wait your turn. And if a boater is foolish enough to cut in line and try to slide into the water ahead of everybody else, all niceties are off. It is not good form—even if you are the vice president of the United States of America—to butt in line. On this day, Cheney was not making friends with those of us who got up early and humped down to the boat ramp. And this was Bush and Cheney country, Republican through and through.

We were ready to launch when the circus arrived. Tires spinning, sirens blaring, lights whirring, and agents springing out of the Hummers and moving over to the queue. Four agents with bomb-sniffing dogs approached.

"Good morning, gentlemen," one of them said politely enough but completely without any form of sincerity in his voice. "The vice president will be putting in this morning so we're going to ask you to hold your positions until we've launched." Already agents were swarming the launch line, looking suspiciously at vehicles, requiring fishermen to open their doors, trunks, hoods, coolers, or anything that could conceivably hide a potentially dangerous weapon. Since we were the next launch, three agents were already poking around our rig. It wasn't sitting right with me.

"Vice president of what?" I asked. And the minute I did that, I not only got a stern glare from my buddies—the "I can't believe you just said that" look—but the agent stopped in his tracks, turned, and came back to me directly.

"Of the United States of America," he said, offering me a clue in his tone that if I so much as blinked wrong, rolled my eyes, or said anything—anything at all—at best, my day might be very miserable, and at worst, I COULD DISAPPEAR.

I'm certain that what happened next has happened to all of us at one time or another on the river. Perhaps, let's say, we've been casting a #24 emerger to a fat brown trout, and let's say we've made a thousand casts and the trout keeps rising, bumping the fly, nudging it, and the one time it slurps the fly, we set too quick or too slow, and without hesitation or consideration for our other brothers and sisters on the water, we let out a rather colorful string of profanities. Fowl lift from the water in fear, large flocks of quail burst from the deep brush and take to the sky, coyotes start howling, and deer bound off at breakneck speed, running for cover. It happens. And the greatest surprise of all is that we thought we offered this unholy prayer quietly to ourselves. It is as great a shock for us to hear such a thing out loud as it must have been to all animalkind. I had such a moment without the expletives.

"Would it be possible to ask the vice president of the United States if we could launch our boat while he's getting rigged up because we don't want to sit around all day?"

I'm a little foggy about the next series of movements because... well, because they happened so quickly. Before the question mark was fully at the end of my sentence, four agents arrived and two dogs—one a Great Dane and one a mutt of some mixed breed—were sniffing us, sniffing our crotches, circling the dory, and pawing around the Suburban. A stunningly beautiful FBI agent approached the back of our vehicle, quickly dropped down to the ground as though she was going to do a series of fingertip pushups, rolled over on her back, and shimmied under the carriage of Gene's rig, looking for explosives. The agent I'd been "chatting" with ordered us to stand back, get away from our rig, and not to move. He particularly singled me out from our crowd. "You," he said, pointing directly at me, "stand on the walkway and don't move so much as an inch." If my buddies could have turned me in for anything at all, I had this gut feeling that they would have done so in a heartbeat.

I have a couple of character flaws (my wife would suggest more than a couple) that I must constantly strive to overcome in my daily life. One is that I have difficulty with authority figures. Actually, it would be more honest to say I have deep-seated aversion to authority figures. And the second is that once I find something to be the least bit funny, regardless of the circumstance and the dangers that might be associated with showing the beginnings of a smile not to mention a smirk or the faint sound of muffled laughter, I'm all in. I simply can't control myself. So in this instance, on this beautiful morning when we were almost on the river before the weight of national security crushed down upon us, these two weaknesses crashed into each other and the perfect storm unfolded. I started to laugh.

Special Agent I Would Love to Kick Your Ass Just Say One More Thing was up in my face in a split second, asking what I found so goddamn funny.

"Nothing," I said, trying desperately not to lose it.

"But you think something's funny, Mr. Wise Guy." We were both stuck in a very bad, B-rated showdown. Did anybody really call anybody else a "wise guy" in this day and age? "You want to share what you find so funny with me?"

"Well," I said, "the reason I was laughing was because when you weren't looking, I stepped off the sidewalk three times." And I started laughing. Uncontrollably.

It would be rather churlish of me to print his reply. Because I am a fly fisherman, I choose to take the high road here, but let me be clear: the act he suggested I perform on myself is almost certainly a physical impossibility.

We were the first boat to roll down the ramp after the vice president and his dog and pony show hit town. At the bottom of the ramp, his team was waiting to cast off. Cheney was rigging up his own fly rod. I liked that. He was wearing neoprene waders in the summer. Bush league—no pun intended. At that moment, he was just another guy on the river, but not. He *could* have been just another guy, and I liked to imagine it was so.

One of our group greeted Cheney by offering up a "Hello, Mr. Vice President—a beautiful day for fly-fishing." He never received so much as a nod in reply. After making a long line of boaters wait for over an hour and a half to cast off, that seemed rather rude to me, so I finally asked him if he was going to fish or just cut bait. He heard that and looked up and scowled at me, and I snapped a picture of him.

My second-grade teacher, Mrs. Kent, who could have been Abe Lincoln in drag, taught me some very important life skills that have remained part of my DNA. They had nothing to do with school; they were bigger than school because they had to do with recess. She made us memorize and practice the following rules:

1.   Do not push or shove in recess line.
2.   Do not cut in front of people.
3.   Do not use your size to bully other students.
4.   Try to make a new friend every day.

I thought about Mrs. Kent's rules as we backed our rig down the ramp. Notwithstanding the fact that I didn't see eye to eye with Cheney on anything other than sharing his appreciation for the deep magic of fly-fishing, I think he missed a very important opportunity that morning. This was his crowd. These were pistol-packing NRA supporters, in a pro-life, anti–gay marriage, drill-for-oil, chop-down-trees state that hadn't voted a Democratic ticket since 1964. Instead of the high drama of sirens, flashing lights, etc., he could have arrived at the ramp, allowed the security system to get set in place, and—surrounded by whatever protective staff was necessary—walked down the line, shook some hands, asked about the fishing conditions, and just done what all fishermen do when they're stuck in such a situation.

Instead, he violated Mrs. Kent's rules. Every single one of them. And had she been around, you could forget about the FBI and Secret Service, little Dick Cheney would have been scolded for his sense of privilege and made to stand in the corner. They were good lessons for me in the second grade, and I don't think they would have hurt the vice president of the United States one bit.

ROCK, PAPER, SCISSORS

I've been a western rivers fly fisherman all my life. So an invitation by the Carstensens to join them at their family home in Martha's Vineyard to fish for striper and bluefish was beyond tempting—it was dangerous. Dangerous, as Alana said, "because you need another excuse to be fly-fishing like a hole in the head."

A poor year of fly-fishing for me would be less than fifty days on the water. Most years, between eighty and one hundred is average. I'm a trout slut, and I admit this without shame. So when the invitation from the Carstensens came, I was definitely in need of another "hole in my head."

But there was real peril in expanding my territory: if I liked fishing in the deeps, chasing big fish in the ocean, my dreamscapes of fishing could easily be expanded to include bone fishing in Belize, big-shouldered browns in New Zealand and Patagonia, steelhead fishing in Iceland, salmon fishing in Scotland, and—closer to home— the seduction of Alaska. I weighed these dangers carefully and after a couple of seconds said, "Absolutely, Terry. We'd love to come!"

I first met Terry Carstensen at a reading by the students of the Sawtooth Writers' Conference. Following the reading, Kranes and I were talking with some Stanley locals when Terry came up and introduced herself. She asked us where we put the faculty members up during our three-week conference.

"Any place that I can find," I said, laughing because the faculty was spread out between lower and upper Stanley.

"My husband and I have been talking it over, and we'd like to offer you our ranch on Crooked Creek for the faculty whenever you hold your conference."

It caught us both by complete surprise. The Carstensens didn't know us at all, but Terry replied by saying she knew the Captain and his wife and that was good enough for them. So for the remainder of the next ten years of the conference, the faculty had access to the splendid accommodations of the ranch on Crooked Creek. Beyond the life of the conference, a few of us have had access to the ranch for steelheading during the month of April. Their generosity to us and to the community of Stanley is beyond compare.

Prior to our departure for Martha's Vineyard I asked the Captain, who would be there too, what we could do for Terry and Hans when we arrived to show our appreciation for their hospitality.

"They love the way we cook. We can cook for them. They'd really like that."

"Done. How will all of this work?" I asked, feeling at a loss for not knowing anything about fishing for striper or bluefish.

"When we get there, Hans will have a boat ready for us and a couple of scotches iced and in hand. We should take the boat out and see what we can do. One night they'll order up a seafood dinner and then one day they'll take us out with guides. They're a couple of brothers, Tim and Mo, that only guide for Terry and Hans. I've been out with them a number of times over the years and they are good at finding fish."

The Captain was right. No sooner had we arrived at the Carstensens' home when cocktails were poured and we made our way to the dock to put off in search of striper and bluefish. Because this was new to me, I asked the obvious. "Exactly what should we be looking for? I mean this is pretty big water."

"Sea gulls and bait balls," the Captain replied. "We'll be looking for any congregation of birds. The bait balls are large and close to the surface so the seagulls prey on them. We'll cast into the boils and land fish."

Breaking out of the inlet, we immediately spied a bait ball and headed directly into the action. Cutting the engine to idle, the Captain gave me quick instructions on casting and stripping the line. The strip, with the rod held parallel to the water, was a simple good, hard set. Instead of lifting the rod into the air while setting a trout, the striper set was counterintuitive to what I'd ever done in my fly-fishing. Within ten minutes after reaching the bait ball— the Captain fishing from the stern and me fishing from the bow— we'd caught and released somewhere in the neighborhood of thirty bluefish. It was exhilarating. But no stripers.

"It's still early in the season, and stripers are more difficult to catch," he said, offering that we'd get into some good-sized ones when we fished the rips. The following day we went out again, with a mutual friend, Tom Koviliche, a former Forest Ranger from the Stanley Basin area who had become a member of the extended Carstensen family. We worked bays, inlets, and open water with moderate success. This saltwater hunting for big fish was growing on me. I could feel the onset of disease coming on. I started dreaming of bone fishing in Florida and chasing tarpon, permit, and stripers in flat-bottomed skiffs.

On our third day, we met Mo and Tim and headed out to open water. The Captain and I went in one boat with Tim and Terry; Hans and Tom went with Mo in the second boat. Torrential rains hit us immediately, and lightning cracked across the sky. Tim thought it would be good to pull into a coved area and wait out the passing storm but we saw a bait ball, and pressured by both of us, he headed into the thick of it. Again we began landing numerous bluefish, one of which we'd been asked to keep for dinner.

When the weather cleared, Tim explained to me that we would try to get into a particular slot of water on a riptide. "We'll position the boat on the edge of the rip where the water curls just before it crashes onto the outgoing tide."

Confused because I couldn't exactly visualize this, I asked, "Do you mean at the point where the returning current will be pushing us into giant waves?"

"Exactly," he said with a smile. I looked at the Captain, who was also smiling.

"Okay," I said, my stomach being tested by the rolling motion of the sea.

Tim kept his head down and we pushed toward water that was keenly sought after by the guides and locals. The foul weather worked to our advantage. By the time we arrived, we were only the second or third boat in the slot.

"This is good," Tim said, positioning us directly toward the breaking waves.

"Get your rod, Metcalf," yelled the Captain.

"You first," I said, offering the spot because the Captain had been instrumental in me receiving the invitation and also I could watch what he was doing—how he was casting and where.

"No. Get your rod and cast," he insisted.

"After you." This had always been a bone of contention with us when we fished together and we were headhunting fish, steelhead in particular.

"I've had a chance to do this for seven years. This is your first time. Get your rod and cast."

"Rock, paper, scissors," I replied. Reluctantly he agreed, and he actually won, throwing down a rock to my scissors. In twenty-plus years it's only the second time this has ever happened. It figured.

It's an odd sensation, steadying a boat in a pattern where the waves are higher than the bow of the boat and staying back from the current to keep from getting pummeled and sucked into swirling waters. It also isn't an easy cast by any means, compounded by a stiff and constant wind blowing into our faces. I studied how the Captain negotiated the cast.

"So, how would you like me to fish this?" I whispered to Tim.

"Stripers are opportunists. They stay low in the water, kind of holding in this area because it's a good food source. We're looking for squid in the curls. If you see a squid, fire into the wave and get ready."

"Okay," I replied. "Ideally, where would you like me to put the fly?"

Tim hesitated for a moment, and I knew exactly what he was thinking: *Can this guy even make a long cast into the wind?* With the bluefish, neither of us needed to make much of a cast. Even in the storm, all we had to do was get our flies into the boil and strip the fly. The feeding frenzy took care of the rest. But here, under these adverse conditions, with exactness required to maximize any success, Tim was thinking—as would any good guide—*I hope to hell this guy can cast or it's going to be a painful morning.* It's the guide's dilemma and it's always a crapshoot when you go out with new clients.

I immediately remembered a client I'd had many years ago who, when asked, told me he'd just started fly-fishing a couple of years before, but that he'd made up for lost time and fished a great deal, proudly remarking that it was "maybe fifteen or twenty times." It was a long day. So I knew what Tim was thinking.

"Fish on!" Captain cried, and he quickly landed a healthy male. "You're up, Metcalf. Remember the set."

Tim offered me an apology as I moved to the bow of the boat. "Listen, I'm sorry about the wind and we can't get closer. It'd be too dangerous."

"But wait until I see a squid, right?" I was double-checking.

"Just... well... maybe with this wind if you can get it close to the curl you might be able to catch a striper."

It was an underwhelming vote of confidence.

"But the perfect cast would be?" I asked firmly.

"Ten to twelve inches behind the squid." There was little hope in his voice.

What Tim could not have known was that I was comfortable casting into the wind. Years of steelhead fishing with the Captain on the Salmon River into howling wind and snow whirls had prepared me well. Granted, it was windy, but nothing like I'd experienced on a yearly basis, and it was warm. Before stripping out some line, I looked at the Captain. He was smiling.

I stripped line out onto the water and watched the slack immediately hold in much the same pattern as the boat. I could, I guessed, be able to shoot a fair amount of line out without concerning myself too much with the possibility it would tangle. This was good. I wasn't prepared for the first squid, and I looked back at Tim. I could feel him roll his eyes. But I did get the line measured, and when the second squid—exhuming seawater and propelling itself in a tapered and streamlined fashion—rode the curl of the break, I fired a cast.

The line shot cleanly no less than a foot behind the squid. The surface exploded as a wide-mouthed striper violently hit the squid. I did as instructed, and set and landed my first striper in less than five minutes. I let out a war cry and looked to Tim and the Captain with a shit-eating grin. I was shaking.

"That scared me half to death!"

"Oh my god," Tim yelled, "that was fucking perfect!" He looked over at the Captain and screamed, "You never told me this guy could cast!"

And the Captain, grinning the knowing grin, replied, "I would have but you never asked me." Tim started laughing. It was the Captain at his best: quiet, understated, and allowing the moment of discovery to belong to both the doubtful guide and the quietly confident dude.

THE MCALLISTER SUPPER CLUB

The McAllister Supper Club, just outside of Ennis, Montana, was a no-nonsense throwback to what we all imagine a supper club might have been like in the late nineteenth century or early twentieth century. It was a good watering hole, and there was always the possibility that any evening a fight could break out in an instant. The ragged fall fly-fishing crew, after floating the Madison and pushing big water on foot for several days, would proper ourselves and head there for dinner. It was a highly anticipated ritual, preceded by a week of drunken chaos, cigar smoking, good whiskey, card playing, lying, and—when we'd worn ourselves dumb—the celebration of each other's company at McAllister's.

The McAllister Supper Club served steaks. Big, broad, thick steaks, and there was very little deliberation about ordering anything else. Of course you could get chicken, but why? Steak; a baked potato smothered with butter, sour cream, and chives; and, after dinner, baked apple pie with a couple of scoops of sinfully rich vanilla ice cream. These were steaks one could brag about. They were flavorful and from local cattle. Bigger than your imagination. Nobody in our group ordered the sixteen-ounce steak; that was an appetizer. Most of us ordered the same thing, year in and year out: the thirty-six-ounce T-bone. Bigger than the plate, certainly bigger than any fish we caught, and the size grew proportionately as we carried these stories with us.

When we all grew up and got adult jobs, the group started to dissipate. People moved away, became parents, and just plain fell into life in all the wonderful and not so wonderful ways that we do. With fewer and fewer of the old guard returning for the fall fly-fishing, our numbers began to decline. For many of the boys it didn't make sense to drive several hundred miles or fly in from the coasts when business and family obligations now occupied our lives. Our fly-fishing trips slowly faded away until it was only the hardcores who ventured to Montana and Idaho for the fall pilgrimage.

I'd still sneak away and fly-fish western water by myself, but Alana, pregnant with our first child, was concerned about me fishing alone. Things could happen to me. I could slip into the river and find myself in a terrible fix. There was no end to our conversations, and I understood her worries. After all, we were expecting a child. Carefully and delicately I presented what I believed to be very good counterarguments, but I just couldn't win.

"But what if you slip and something happens? You get swept downriver?"

"That could happen any day I go to the Provo or Green River. It has, and I just swim to the bank, dry off, and continue fishing."

"But what if a grizzly crosses your path?"

"It's late fall. They'll be in hibernation."

"But what if there's a rogue grizzly?"

"Then I'd be in serious trouble."

"See?"

One year, to solve the problem, I suggested she join me for a long weekend in Ennis, Montana. We'd rent a small cabin, and she could read the stack of books piled on her bedstand with a big fire going and I could fly-fish. Plus—and I'm certain this was the big-ticket item—I would take her out to dinner at the McAllister Supper Club! Taaa dahhhh!

I hadn't been to the supper club in a few years and it had transformed into, well, a more modernized supper club: red-and-white-checkered tablecloths, small jelly-jar glass vases with a plastic flower on each table, and an atmosphere that seemed genuinely civilized.

There was country-western on the radio when we entered, and we were promptly seated at a two-top with a good view of all goings on.

Our waitress—a cowgirl named Lacey, no older than eighteen— brought us menus and dropped off a large pitcher of cold water. Alana studied the menu carefully.

"Things have changed around here," I said, wistfully reminiscing about the old days. "There would never have been a plastic rose on the table."

"Look at the menu. It's too funny."

I did a quick study and didn't find anything that different except the inclusion of wine on the menu. "They have wine."

"Look again. Carefully."

This time I noticed, and we both started laughing. "I think you're probably the first to notice that on the menu."

All Entrees are Ala Carte and come with the following:
Soup or salad
Baked potato or spaghetti
Choice of dessert

We ordered. Alana wanted a glass of wine with dinner so I inquired about the wine list.

"We actually don't got a wine list," Lacey replied with a big smile. "We only got two kinds."

"Okay, tell me about them."

"One is red and one is yellow."

Alana looked at me from across the table and smiled. "I don't know about you, honey, but I think I'll stay with the red." Our smiles broadened when Lacey added, "Good call. That's what most people get."

"Lacey, what kind of red wine do you have?" I asked out of curiosity.

"We got two kinds. Screw or cork."

"With your permission?" I nodded to Alana, and she gave me the "go ahead" nod. "We'll go with the cork."

"Excellent choice," Lacey replied, disappearing into the kitchen to place our orders.

Our meals arrived before the wine. Lacey, anticipating my question, said, "It should be done by now. I'll go bring it out."

She returned pushing a small cart covered with a tablecloth and a clear, ice-filled Plexiglas tub about the size of a deep-sided steamer pan, our bottle of corked wine sitting on the top.

"Sorry for the wait," she said apologetically, "but somebody didn't put the corkscrew back where it was supposed to go so I just opened it. But it's real cold. I iced it up really good."

And it was. When she poured us a glass—no sense wasting time tasting it—the wine came out of the bottle the consistency of a Slurpee. We gave her a thumbs-up because to say anything would have sent us both into a laughing fit.

It began to snow outside and some good belt-buckle-rubbing music came on over jukebox. An elderly couple we'd been watching during dinner got up to dance. The man's name was Carl. We knew that because it was carved in the back of his belt. Carl announced to the room that he and "the little lady" were celebrating their fortieth wedding anniversary. Carl was about 6'4", cowboy boney, wearing a wide-brim cowboy hat, slim Wrangler jeans, and a big rodeo belt, and the little lady was just the opposite. But it seemed to work.

The rest of the world was outside the McAllister Supper Club that evening, and we weren't. Instead, we were where we should be, having just eaten a wondrously delicious dinner, dancing cheek to cheek, and swaying to a Patsy Cline tune with the world of parenthood in front of us. And it just felt right.

OVER THE EDGE

————

Here's the problem: I fly-fish. And when I am not fly-fishing, I think about fly-fishing. I think of great hatches. I think about trout. Big, fat, hungry trout. Which means I'm thinking about fly-fishing all the time. It's a vicious circle. I know this.

So when my friend Gene called and mentioned he had a great opportunity and it dealt with fly-fishing in Idaho, my head went to mush. Turns out what he actually said and what I heard were very different.

"Anyway," Gene said, "there will be five of us, two catarafts, a guide, and some incredible water with big trout—cutthroat, rainbows, and cutbow hybrids. The best part is that we won't see another person all day long." He paused before adding, "But it might be a little dangerous." This he said with understatement and as an afterthought, but I wouldn't have heard it anyway.

Instead, what I heard was this: "fly-fishing...big trout, lots of them...nobody else on the river." What I didn't hear were the finer details: (1) Not many people attempt this trip because it is, after all, dangerous, (2) We will have to lash the catarafts to ropes and lower them down a one-thousand-foot slide, (3) There are often rattlesnakes on the ledges, (4)...not to mention some pretty good whitewater. "But otherwise," and this is where my real hearing returned, "we should see some fantastic country and catch some fat trout. Are you interested?"

"I'm already packed." Gene knows this is true because we've fished together before, and he knows I am never without a fly rod, waders, a vest, and a complete set of clothing in case Alana locks me out of the house or moves suddenly in the middle of the night. And there have been those days when fishing time dissolves and gets lost in river time. When the "I'll be home around six or sevenish" turns into a late-night, side-of-the-road truck-stop phone call that doesn't end pretty. In the end, even with offering details about the hatch, the number of trout, the way the sky looked, or how a speckled phantom seduced you into staying longer than you should have, there is not much you can say. So when I tell Gene to count me in, he knows I will be the last seat in the cataraft with no questions asked.

On the drive from Salt Lake City to Irwin, Idaho, where we would meet our guide and rendezvous with the other members of the fishing expedition, Gene began to fill in the details. Up to this point the specifics had been very vague, something like, "We'll drive down a private dirt road on some farmland to the edge of a cliff, hook up the rafts onto climbing ropes, lower them over the edge, and drop down into the water. We'll try not to flip them over or lose them off the cliff. If we can keep them from flipping in the rapids, we'll catch some great trout."

To get specific answers from any fisherman, you have to ask specific questions. Even then, it's a crapshoot. So I ask the obvious: "What stretch of water are we talking about here, Gene?"

For a moment, Gene looked at me like we'd had this conversation before, which we had, but because he knows I think in terms of trout and not necessarily in terms of geography, he went over it again. "The Teton Narrows just outside Driggs, Idaho. We'll put in on the Bitch Creek Slide and drop down to where the Teton River and Bitch Creek intersect, above where the Teton Dam blew out in '76. The water might be a little tricky. It's low this year, which changes the personality of the river."

This I understood because I used to be a river guide and knew how reckless and capricious water could be. But it was a straightforward answer, better than the one I was able to give to my wife.

"Okay," I answered, "it sounds great."

Our guide for the trip was Gene's son, Chris Jensen, who worked for the Palisades Creek guide service. Chris was the youngest guide to be licensed on the South Fork of the Snake River. He has probably made the Teton Narrows run as often as any other guide on the river, and he knew this water well.

We rendezvoused up with our fishing companions at a motel, loaded up the gear into two rigs, and took off for the Teton River. If I tried to give directions to the spot it would sound something like a kidnapper giving directions for a money drop: "Pass through Driggs; turn off on this little dirt road; follow a small, bumpy, rutted private path on a potato farmer's land; then make a turn toward the edge of the cliff and you're there! Leave the money there in a brown paper bag. Make sure nobody's around. Got it?" Sure. Sure. So suffice to say, I could not find that place again if my life depended on it.

Once we got there, we roped up the cataraft, cinched ourselves onto a belay line, took a deep breath, and started over the cliff. To my left, straight out about two hundred feet, an osprey rocked gently on air currents. Its long wings and black mask confirmed it was an adult on the hunt. It wasted no energy, only occasionally feathering its wings. I do not look up often when I am fly-fishing because I am usually so focused on the water. But on this day I was acutely aware that this bird and I were in a splendid dance together. It was the dance of trout. The difference is that the osprey was already studying the river, looking for trout some one thousand feet below, and I couldn't even see the water. I could hear it off in the distance, a faint grumbling sound. But until we worked our catarafts carefully down the slide, over a series of boulders and through some very tight rock walls, the moment and the river belonged to this bird of prey. The osprey gave a clear cry, tucked its wings back into a diving position, and disappeared into the Teton Narrows.

I was relieved to discover the canyon wall was not completely vertical. It was steep, but not at such an angle that it required us to be on belay for the entire descent. We pushed, pulled, and belayed the catarafts down the slide and off the wall. The terrain was a combination of dirt and gravel interrupted by trees, boulders, and steep ledges. It was dusty and dirty and the thought crossed my mind that a rappel straight down the canyon wall might have been easier. When we got to the last cliff, one that dropped down twenty or so feet, the guides shouted for us to let loose the catarafts, and we watched them crash onto a gravel bar at the river's edge. Two oarsmen, already at the bottom, made certain we didn't lose them.

Covered in dirt, ringed in perspiration, and cotton-mouthed, we took a quick inventory of the descent. Gene sported a gash under his right eye after being catapulted into the tail end of a cataraft. One of the guide bars on the lead cataraft was bent over but could be easily hammered back into position. I replaced a broken lens filter on my camera. All in all, we were none the worse for wear.

After a brisk dip in the water, we decided to move up and fish the junction where Bitch Creek Canyon and the Teton River intersected each other. Crazy Charlie and I headed up Bitch Creek while Gene, Bobby, and Green fished the deep runs and swift riffles upriver on the Teton.

It didn't take long before we hooked into trout. There was a PMD hatch, so I worked the surface while Crazy Charlie used an attractor pattern dry fly with a zebra midge dropper. Both techniques produced trout immediately. Almost every trout blew out of the water, danced, and then headed for any type of structure that might disengage the fly. Given the choice, I could have spent the remainder of the day working my way up the canyon, happily headhunting trout and being virtually alone on water that is seldom fished. It took Chris's promise of more trout downriver and a reminder that we hadn't "really started the fishing part of the trip yet" to gather us all back to the catarafts.

All day long we concentrated on fishing the banks using a variety of attractor patterns and terrestrials, the usual summer suspects:

grasshoppers, ants, beetles, Turk's tarantulas, and golden stones, and when we couldn't tease any trout on the surface, we went underneath with bead-headed hare's ears, prince nymphs, Copper Johns, and tungsten zebra midges. Between the Bitch Creek Slide and the Spring Hollow boat ramp, the river is marked by a series of four rapids followed by wide-open, flat, slow-moving water. The upper stretch of the float, before the first set of rapids, is perhaps the most classic of any canyon trout water. Undercut banks, boulders, riffles, and an abundance of aquatic plant life provide excellent cover for trout.

This is the thing. I honestly can't remember if we stopped for lunch or took a break from fishing or not. I'm fairly certain we must have, but I honestly can't write this as truth. I'd become disengaged from the social aspect of the trip and fully engaged in everything about the water: the vibrant braids of what I call mermaid hair undulating with the current, so often looking like a trout holding in a seam; above, the call of the occasional osprey in search of food; the absolute privilege of being here at this moment, a guest on this secluded section of the Teton River.

At the end of the day we oared in fading light toward the boat ramp. I couldn't help but become a bit nostalgic about the day. Circumstance afforded us unusual access and privacy not found these days on many waters. We did not see a single other person on the river, and I thought about my early days as a young man, tramping about the rivers of northern Utah and Idaho. So often I would have miles of river to myself—seldom, if ever, crossing paths with another fly fisherman. And when I did, we'd always visit, exchange a fly or two, and then move on our way. I understood then, even in my youth, that this solitude would not last forever, but I have held these river memories deep inside my bones. I take a risk here by writing that, at one point, as we traveled the fading light of eventide, I looked back over my shoulder to the bank and thought, just for an instant, that I saw myself as a young man, casting to a rising trout in the slick skim of water.

PHANTOM

Part of fly-fishing's narcotic effect is being surprised by the unexpected: trout hiding in the most unpredictable spots, an irrigation ditch high above one of the great deep pools on the Provo River that holds tremendous carp and misplaced brown trout, or the crash of a moose thundering out from dense brush and plowing through the water no more than one hundred yards from where you have been casting tiny dry flies to rising trout on Currant Creek.

In many of the places I have fished there are concerns of a more dangerous nature. Grizzlies fear nothing. They are at the top of the food chain. A couple of years ago, one of the owners of TroutHunter Lodge was walking home to his cabin not far from his shop when he was attacked by a grizzly. He survived the attack but lost a finger. I was in the shop earlier that day and had him help me select some flies for Henry's Fork. When I returned in the afternoon to purchase some tapered leader, I heard about the attack. The story was a confused narrative but he was probably saved because of his dogs, who attacked the grizzly, and a good friend who knew what to do.

Of course there are nature's perils too: lightning on open water; the possibility of flash floods in the landscape of southern Utah, where deep canyons can explode into desert tsunamis; snow when one doesn't expect it; current so swift that one errant step during wading could prove fatal. I know of these risks, and still I am drawn to wild waters.

This story belongs someplace else, perhaps in a category all its own. It begins simply enough on the lower Provo River, with a crowd of fly fishermen working a hatch. Some days, certain runs of the Provo from Sundance to Cable Hole tend to be stacked with both trout and trout hunters. I try to avoid those days if I can, and when I find myself compressed by my fellow anglers, I rethink the feeding habits of trout and try to make adjustments to my schedule. I arrive earlier or later than most, and I work water that some might consider too pedestrian or unlikely to produce trout. Granted, there might be fewer trout, but that has seldom mattered to me. I like the seclusion and most often can stick a trout or two. It's enough.

I recall an afternoon when I decided to get onto the water and mix it up with the crowds. For one reason or another I arrived much later than anticipated. I contemplated turning back. Instead, I pulled into the parking lot by the bridge midway up the canyon. It was near impossible to find a parking space, which told me that I'd missed a fabulous hatch. I was disappointed in myself for letting life get in the way of trout.

As I was gearing up, fly fishermen were coming off the river, sporting broad smiles, backslapping each other, and speaking in the excited and often exaggerated language of people who have had a banner day on the water. I knew a number of these folks, and a few of them, as they reached the parking area, chided me for missing the most "epic" hatch in the last twenty years. Normally such banter wouldn't annoy me, but in this case I knew exactly what I'd missed and didn't need to be reminded. I wanted to say something snotty like, "How would you know what the fishing was like twenty years ago, dipshit?"

Instead, I remembered a time when my friend Jim Bradley and I had fished a private stretch of water at just the same time as the current hatch. The day had been splendid, with a consistent, steady flow of decent-sized browns. Since the private water we were fishing, 1,000 Peaks, was some distance from our homes in Salt Lake, we'd intended to get off the water early enough to make the drive back while it was still light. It did not happen, and soon we found ourselves staying beyond dusk and into darkness. The fishing continued to get better and better; we even considered staying the night and switching over to big streamers and mice, but we both knew where that would have led. Both of us had been married before, and then divorced; we couldn't afford to do it again.

Thinking about that day, I began to feel better about my tardiness on the Provo. Might I be fortunate enough to find similar circumstances this evening? Just the thought of it propelled me down to the water.

The flats where I wanted to fish were abandoned, and from my vantage point I could see only a couple of other fishermen getting off the river. That meant I had the water to myself. I sat on the bank and studied the water, looking for noses and boils but saw nothing. I considered what the day must have looked like with a river stacked full of fishermen, leaving trout with sore lips and bellies full of food. It was not a promising or encouraging thought. But I'd long ago learned to never assume anything when it comes to trout. The more I fished, the less I felt I actually knew.

The temperature was beginning to drop and the air was damp. I was thinking about returning to my rig to grab a lightweight jacket when I saw the first slurp, followed by another. Soon the river began to look as though it was lightly raining; slurp upon slurp, and the trout were keying in on fall caddis. I tied a fly on and slid into the water and began casting. Oh, how heaven rewards those who wait. I was in the zone.

A light fog blanketed the water and hung like ghostly vapor moving downriver. I returned to the bank, sat down, snipped off a shredded caddis, and tied on another. As I ginked the fly I heard, directly across from where I had been fishing, the whish of a fly line in the air. It had to be another fly fisherman, but an evening mist prevented me from seeing across the river so I dismissed the idea immediately. Besides, had another soul climbed into the water I most assuredly would have seen or heard him walking upriver from the bridge. But then I heard a "Yes!" and the slapping of trout on water. *Curious,* I thought, but it didn't bother me. If there was somebody else on the river it was comforting; the mist and encroaching darkness can make the imagination play games with a person's mind.

A window slit in the fog allowed me a glance across the river. I am aware that what I write next might seem contrived or mythological. I saw a tall, handsome Native American man, much younger than myself, fishing with a bamboo fly rod and making beautiful looping casts out onto the water. I called across the water, "A great night?" He nodded his head in agreement and then turned back to the business of casting. The fog swallowed us both up.

For the next hour or so we seemed to parallel each other, casting upriver, sharing a mystical night of trout, hearing each other's fish play out a run. We'd gotten to a spot where it was fairly easy to wade from one side to the other. Tucked in the back of my vest I had a thermos of hot coffee. It would be easy enough for one of us to wade to the other side and share a cup. It was getting colder and damper, and I was shuddering uncontrollably. Maybe the coffee would help but I realized, given the situation, it was time.

"I've got some hot coffee. You want a cup?" I shouted.

I heard nothing in return and called again. I became aware that the whishing of line had stopped. I'd made what I considered to be a friendly offer and it seemed only reasonable that I get some sort of response in return. I got out of the water, unslung my vest, and poured myself a cup. It wasn't hot but it tasted good. Even with the infusion of coffee I was trembling with the cold and damp. Regardless of this splendid night, I'd have to leave the water soon.

The layers of mist began to peel away and lift off the water. I searched the other side of the river to no avail. There was nobody upriver or downriver fishing. Of this I am certain. What I am uncertain of, however, is whether this truly happened or whether that man was an illusion that I have shaped into a truth. In the end, who can really say?

TRUTHS AND REAL LIES

I get the Christmas card in June. At first I don't think too much of it because after twenty-two years of living in the Holladay area at the same address, my family and I have packed everything up and moved to downtown Salt Lake City to become *townies*. The mail follows us in its own mystical way. Sometimes it gets forwarded properly and sometimes it doesn't, but I recognize the chicken scratching on the outside of this envelope so I am extremely curious. Bold, dark indigo-ink scribble—this lopsided cursive handwriting is that of a former professor of English and an old fly-fishing buddy of mine, P. Sully. In the bottom, left-hand corner are carefully printed words: "TOP SECRET!" I hold the envelope to the light just to see if anybody has tampered with the seal. It looks untouched. In my office, with the doors closed, I take an ivory-handled letter opener and gut the envelope.

It is an exquisitely hand-painted card of a brook trout, illustrated by watercolorist Joseph Timelier. Sully has drawn a red Santa hat on the crown of the trout. The card is informative. Both Sully and his lovely wife are doing well in Port Townsend. Most mornings, while his wife paints landscapes of the rugged Washington coastline, Sully and his black lab walk along the beach picking up driftwood.

And here,
he wrote,

I am studying the songs of fish.

The secret comes at the very end of the card:

Have taken great interest in the LDS Plaza issue. It's been on the tube up here. Renewed my ACLU card but this has nothing to do with 'free speech'... it is about fishing. I have had these dreams of late. They are always the same. On the first night of a full moon, the trout make their way down from City Creek Canyon into the Reflective Pond at Mormon Temple. You must go fish these trout. This is my last great fishing secret.

I have been friends with Sully for nearly forty years, and I have never known him to lie about fly-fishing. It is not in his nature. At the same time, he is a fly fisherman, and that places him in the elemental position of being prone to exaggeration.

I read the card to Alana and ask her what she thinks. After she stops laughing, she reminds me of the time Sully and I fished the Provo River until *dark thirty* because of a prolific caddis hatch. On the way home, in the borrowed jeep of a former attorney general of the state of Utah, we ran out of gas. Still in our waders, we hitchhiked into town, purchased a red plastic gallon-sized gas can from Kmart, filled it up, made our way back to the rig, primed the carburetor, pushed the rig until we could pop the clutch to get it started, and limped into the Salt Lake Valley at first morning light.

"Do you remember what you told me?" she asks. "Who you said you fished with that night, you and Sully?"

"Of course I do," I reply, a little on the defensive side. "The ancestors of the great trout, the native people."

"Ghosts," she says. "There is a difference. 'Ghosts that disappeared into a thick fog.'"

"So you didn't believe me?"

When she gives me the "Look, honey, you are, after all, a fly fisherman—need I say more?" look, I drop the subject instantly. Fly-fishing gets under the skin. It isn't for everybody. And the more one fly-fishes, the more one realizes there is a wider correspondence to the great secrets of life. If one fishes long enough on the great trout waters, the rivers will eventually open up windows of great enlightenment.

What happens in those pure moments, in those windows, is something profound and sacred. Colors thicken. The sound of water has its own chorus against the thick, broad backs of stone, and life hangs on in a delicate balance through the press of water. In a sense, one leaves the familiar world behind and enters into the transcendence of a dream state. It is a seam of experience common to those who meditate deeply. Mind and body become separated and cross over into dimensions that can't be edited by normal conventions. Knowing this experience is what allowed me, years ago, to understand when my uncle, the successful stockbroker, arrived home early from work, packed up his fly rods and waders into a waterproof duffle bag, withdrew all his money from a local bank, and asked me to drive him to the Salt Lake International Airport. When I asked him where he was going, he told me he was headed for Scotland to fly-fish for the Loch Ness Monster.

"Think of it," he said to me as I walked him up to the departing gate, "and then imagine doing it!"

"Do you really believe?"

But before I could ask him anything else, he vanished, disappearing into a crowded terminal. We never saw him again. Occasionally I would receive a postcard from exotic places like Urquhart Castle or the Loch of Firth. Sometimes just rough sketches of Nessie or other kraken with short anecdotal notes:

Locals use fish finders and deep-water jigs to fish for Nessie. I have gone to spey casting and dry flies. I will need both hands to land her if I should hook into her.

Postcards from Loch Morar, where he fished for Morag; and another from Loch Lochy, where he fished for Lizzie; and then the last—and this surprised everybody—from Patagonia, in the remote mountain wilderness surrounding Nahuel Huapi Lake, where he fished for the great Argentine monster Nahuelito. And then the postcards stopped arriving.

I MET A woman once who could lift trout out of a stream with her bare hands. She had learned the art of "guddling" from a Navajo medicine man. It was an exquisite fall day, and I was walking the golden brush–lined banks of the Price River. Having had little success on the water, I climbed a hill and decided to take a short nap. I slid easily into a river sleep, the chorus of rock and water disarming me, making me drowsy.

I heard her voice first. She sang an offering, I suspected, to the fish gods—a ritual chanting. I watched her crawl along the tall wheatgrass to the edge of the river and slide, as seductively as an otter or mink, into the Price River. From my vantage point on the hill I could see three or four plump trout upriver from her. Slowly, very deliberately, she would slide one hand underneath the head of the trout and the other just beneath its tail until the whole trout was cradled in her embrace. With blinding speed she would snatch the trout out of the water and hold it high over her head, cold water spilling down her arms in silver rivulets. Gently she would kiss each trout and return it delicately to the icy water, where it scurried back to the emerald depths of shadow and light.

I stayed in the trees, out of sight, all day and tracked her up the river. Toward the end of the afternoon, she built a fire out of dried aspen wood and watched as it burned into a pile of glowing embers. She combed the banks of the river, pulling wild onions from the earth. From a small side channel she picked fresh watercress, asparagus, and mint leaves. Afterwards, she quickly caught and gutted two fat trout. Into their cavities she stuffed the wild onions, mint, and watercress. She wrapped the trout and asparagus inside aluminum foil, raked back the coals with a stick, and buried the bundle deep in the coals. While the trout cooked, she took off her clothes and dove into a shimmering sweep of the Price River.

A FULL MOON hangs radiantly over the reflective pond in the Temple Square Plaza. For the past two hours I have been well camouflaged, crouched under a giant copper-colored cauldron, a seasonal planter box that looks like a spaceship or some Mayan sacrificial fount. Foot traffic has ceased. A clean-up crew walks lazily around the plaza, occasionally stopping to pick up a scrap of paper or stab a Styrofoam cup. A short, stocky man walks within inches of me. I could reach out and touch him, scare him to death. He finds a quarter, bends over with effort, picks it up, and gives a little shout. He sounds like Bart Simpson.

I'm thinking how stupid this must seem and I'm beginning to feel fairly ridiculous—a full-grown man dressed in a fishing vest, a Winston bamboo rod rigged and ready to go, a #20 Adams tied to 6x tippet. Shortly past midnight I hear a whirring sound and gates— gates that are hidden during the day from the public—rise up from the flowerbeds and interlock into each other. I feel trapped. I'm trying to think of an easy way out. There is no way. My eye is drawn to the reflective pond. The slick glass mirror of water reflects the LDS Temple and moon back into themselves in an exquisite quintessence of light. It is a still-life photograph. A moment of perfection. Ever so slightly, a dimple beneath the surface of the water riffles the image then dissolves. Soon another dimple, and then another. The reflective pond and moon metamorphose into the rolling shoulders of monolithic trout rising to a hatch. I break from the brush, singularly focused on the trout, my casting arm working feverishly to let out line in graduated increments, and my first cast—perfect— and I set the barbless hook too delicately and the trout somersaults in the air, spitting out the fly.

Behind me I hear a wonderful throaty laugh followed by the rich scent of a single-leaf Cuban cigar. "Buck fever," he says, moving from the shadow and shaking his head. It is Mark Twain, in a cream-colored, three-piece linen summer suit, with a split cane rod at the ready. Behind him and closing the distance to the trout pond is Madame Curie, and to her side, having difficulty tying on a fly, Albert Einstein. Sigmund Freud and Buddha are in deep discussion about the art of roll casting while Joan of Arc and Harriet Tubman stand side by side, casting into a boil of trout. Martin Luther King Jr. and Brigham Young admire each other's reels while Rabbi Hillel and the Prophet Muhammad exchange dry flies. Chief Geronimo makes room for Wild Bill Hickok. Soon there is silence. Only the whispers of fly line can be heard across the night as the spidery silver threads of leader and tippet crisscross against the moon's brilliant light. And I know this is not reality. Some of it is and some of it isn't, but it *is* a perfect moment of magic and mystery beyond all reason, drifting softly into Zen, with the promise of possibility.

URBAN ANGLING

Sometimes, when river levels are too high or the opportunity to slip out of work early to wet a line isn't on the horizon, an idea is hatched out of necessity. It's like one of those wonderful moments on the river when a big brown slashes out of the most improbable water, slams into your fly, strips you to the backing, and snaps off the tippet in the blink of an eye. And before you can cry out, "Fish on!" it is off, disappearing deep into the secret place where trout hide. You shake your head and laugh because it was so unexpected. That's the kind of trout heroin that draws you to the water day after day.

One of my favorite fly-fishing partners, David Kempner, was also a marvelous high school history teacher. Whenever we'd fish together he'd give me a history lesson of some sort. I'd get these lessons whether I was in need of them or not. On one such occasion, returning from the Provo River, he began waxing about the lazy summers of his youth.

"When I was a kid and Kennecott Copper was on strike, my father used to work for Scott Avenue Fish Hatchery to make ends meet. Whenever they were stocking fish, I'd get a phone call from the old man and he'd tip me off to where they were dumping the fish. My job was to get my fishing pole, climb on my bike, and be there when they dumped the fish. I always caught my limit and that put food on the table during the strikes."

Kempner began reciting a litany of sites he used to fish that were all within striking distance from his home. Naming one fishing spot led to naming the next, until pretty soon the two of us had composed a substantial list of fishing holes, all within the Salt Lake City region. Although we often had different names for spots, once we got through pinpointing the locations on a map, we realized we'd both crisscrossed and fished the same waters growing up.

Following this nostalgic journey, our conversation turned to the good old days, when fish seemed bigger and more plentiful, the deer were easier to find, and pheasant and game birds could be spooked anywhere there was an open field. We lamented the disappearance of these fields and of farmland that had been replaced by strip malls, unimaginative housing developments, and parking lots. But the question that continued to nag us was this: What, if anything, was still fishable within the city limits? And there, in a nutshell, is the danger of fishing with a history teacher. Always asking questions; always planting seeds.

On a brisk fall morning, when I was certain our wives could have found something more productive for both of us to be doing, Kempner and I met for breakfast at Over the Counter, a favorite greasy spoon, and planned out our strategy. Both of us always had our fly rods tucked away and ready to fish at a moment's notice, so we left the restaurant and began retracing some of our favorite fishing spots.

Together we spent several days bushwhacking our way through parking lots, office spaces, and apartment complexes that intersected the borders of small streams and agricultural ditches, in search of trout. And although much of the water we remembered had been channeled underground, we found some at almost every stop. What surprised us was not so much how the landscape had changed over our lifetimes, but that in many of the areas, even in areas of heavy urban development, fish survived. For that reason alone, it was in many ways an encouraging and promising adventure.

But seeing fish and actually being able to fish to them are two completely different matters. On 3300 South and 700 East, one of the busiest intersections in Salt Lake, there is a triangular building, a Kinko's Copy Center, which has a concrete-walled irrigation canal on the north side of the structure. The canal held trout of decent size.

Quietly creeping up on the water, staying low so our shadows wouldn't spook anything, we spotted rainbow trout in a feeding channel—exactly where one would expect. Several trout within the six-to-ten-inch range darted off when they saw the slightest movement, but an exceptionally large rainbow trout, perhaps fourteen or fifteen inches, hung at the maw of a conduit that channeled water under the six-lane road. It was slurping dry flies—terrestrials, I suspected—as if it were in the backyard of a pristine conservancy. There was a "No Fishing" sign posted on the side of the Kinko's that, for the sake of history, I decided to ignore. Kinko's might have owned the property, but they did not own the water. Kempner, a more rational and civilized man, thought it wasn't such a good idea. With my tiny six-foot Orvis fly rod, I could make a cast without stepping on Kinko's property. I returned to the car, tied on a small ant pattern, made three false casts, and shot the line about three feet under the bridge. The cast was adequate and the rainbow struck hard but immediately went under the conduit and snapped me off. Before Kempner had a chance to lecture me, I was heading back to the car, my heart racing like that of the fifteen-year-old boy who had once fished these spaces freely and openly.

Diagonally across the street, a parking lot and shopping center covered some of the city's great natural springs. Artesian springs still bubble up on the north side of a Rite Aid and there is an abundance of fresh watercress that lines the banks. Trout find safe haven around the discarded tires and shopping carts that litter the water. Through a chain-link fence we could see a narrow road that would give us access. Slingshot casts would be mandatory given the heavy brush and canopy of trees covering the water. Kempner had no inclination to fish this stretch but I made a mental note to return at a later date when there weren't so many people in the mix. Though I knew I might have to compete with some of the late-night graffiti artists because the wall was often tagged.

Our next foray into the world of urban angling was Spring Run, a wonderful mecca from both of our boyhood days, when we could pack a sandwich and a canteen of water, and dissolve into the wilderness of our imaginations within a dozen blocks of our own backyards. Beginning on the northeast corner of the intersection of Van Winkle Expressway and 900 East, this run meanders southwest under a large culvert pipe, dumps into a holding pool, and then becomes part of Big Cottonwood Creek. A restaurant west of Spring Run has a long stretch of smooth water paralleling its outdoor seating area. Easily fishable and approachable from the rear of the restaurant, this water held—to our great surprise—rainbow and brown trout. Farther west, I made casts up over Van Winkle Expressway, much to the amazement of the many drivers hell-bent toward downtown Salt Lake City. (*Cautionary note:* It is imperative to time the back cast between traffic lights. Hooking an SUV screaming by at 50 mph presents a serious set of problems on many levels. The possibility of landing such a vehicle is remote, not to mention the difficulty of finding a net large enough to hold the catch and, of course, the most obvious enigma is how to properly release a ton-and-a-half vehicle once you have it to the net.)

Following that stretch of creek, Kempner and I crossed the road and walked through a diversion pipe that spilled into a wide-open tree-lined pond. This was a manmade pond attached to a condo project. The spot held gigantic carp, browns, and rainbows, not to mention at least a dozen decent-sized koi.

Two phantoms snapped off Kempner's 6x tippet without ever surfacing. I would like to believe that they were brown trout but more than likely they were carp. Still, the thought of being able to hook into something large enough to snap tippet was exhilarating.

We found trout in a pretty thin stretch of water on a Frisbee golf course in Holladay, and more trout in the spill-off from Sugarhouse

Park that runs into a newly developed shopping center. Excited by our discoveries, finding fish at almost all stops, we decided to stop in at the Tap Room for a quick beer before playing the trump card of all urban angling trump cards: the Little Cottonwood as it flows around the Cottonwood Mall.

We decided that our best chance for catching big fish (relatively speaking) would be here. West of the mall's parking lot is a rather long stretch of water that snakes from Cottonwood Canyon through some very beautiful established neighborhoods and along a large parking area for retail stores. From there, the stream cuts under a highway and runs for almost equal distance on the other side of the road.

We both felt there would be trout. As we pulled on our waders and rigged our fly rods, we immediately began to draw onlookers. The appearance of fly fishermen in a parking lot was met with a mixture of disbelief and polite wonderment. Using a six-and-a-half foot, two-weight rod, I hooked into and—after a good fifteen minutes during which I had very little control over matters—landed a twenty-four-inch carp. Fearing that I might have exhausted this prehistoric monolith, and facing the prospect of having to resuscitate the carp before releasing it, I quickly removed my fly and began to massage the fish. The moment it was free of my fly and back in the water, it simply shrugged its shoulders, slipped from my grasp, and lazily disappeared into the depths of a deep pool.

Kempner caught a couple of small crappie and a brown trout of some measure. Using a tungsten bead-head chocolate dropper, or zebra midge, I landed a catfish. A favorite steelhead fly of mine was powerfully effective at hooking carp, and with small rods the fight was substantial. In all, we managed to land five different species of fish, two of which were not native to this stretch of water. (I will reserve my thoughts on *dumpers*, those who infiltrate waters with nonnative species, for another book.)

As interesting as fishing the creek was, the most engaging element of the day was visiting with people who wandered over to the embankment to watch us fish. Astonished to find a couple of derelicts casting into murky water, the dialogue almost always began with a question: "Are there fish in that water?"

"Yes," we would reply, and then if they hung around long enough, we'd invariably hook into some mysterious apparition. The sight of a giant carp thrashing in the water, steadily bending a rod close to the breaking, drew wondrous cries of celebration. A vast majority of the people who visited with us began recalling their own personal experiences catching fish within the city limits. It seemed people took great comfort knowing that fish still punctuated pockets of urban water, and that their memories of doing much the same thing Kempner and I did in our youth were not totally forgotten.

In the several urban sojourns I took with Kempner and other fly-fishing lunatics, we covered a great deal of the city's waterways. Still, there is much to be explored across the valley floor. What began as a rather cavalier idea evolved into something larger, and instigated some rather big questions: What would it take in terms of time and resources to try to reclaim these waters? Could they be made fishable again?

Is there anything more splendid than driving home after a grueling day at work, rolling down the window, pulling off the road, slipping out of your city skin, and sliding into a pair of waders in search of trout? And with that first cast, perhaps only a half mile from your living room, feeling the knots in your back dissolve into the image of dancing trout?

Such are the worthy dreams of madmen and visionaries.

TENKARA

When 9/11 exploded into the world our son, John, was deep into his seventh-grade camping trip in the red rock landscape of southern Utah. My wife and I are old enough to remember where we were and what we were doing on the day John F. Kennedy died, and we wondered what our son was doing on that morning. The desert landscape refuses cell phone service, so the innocence he and his classmates took into the canyons would be the same innocence they returned with to the gate of civilization. Then, somehow and in some way, without any comfort, they would hear of this tragedy. The world's axis tilted while they explored the ancient landscape of the Anasazi Indians, flexing their muscles, imagining what it might have been like to roam the desert—hunting, foraging, and engaging themselves completely in the wild. We wanted and hoped to be the first to talk with him but we knew that would probably not be the case. It was the bus driver, John said, that told them all that war had been declared on the United States. As a seventh grader, and now as a thirty-year-old man, John has always been a sensitive and wise soul. We struggled like all parents to find a way to make sense of such a senseless act, but in the end it is impossible.

Shortly after 9/11, the committee members of the Japanese Fulbright Memorial Exchange Program and their American counterparts were trying to decide whether or not to cancel the program, which was slated to commence on October first. I was one of the 150+ American teacher/scholars that had been selected to spend two weeks in Japan, visiting public and private schools in an exchange of ideas regarding each country's educational system. We'd all been informed that these discussions were taking place and that, due to issues regarding the safety of American citizens traveling abroad, the exchange program might be cancelled. Several of us wrote letters encouraging the committee members to stay the course, and in the end they decided not to be deterred. They did offer participants the option to withdraw from the exchange if they felt in any danger, and a handful did. I could not fault them for the decision. It was such a complicated and uncertain time.

Security was heightened when we arrived in Tokyo. Each Fulbright member had been assigned to a particular prefecture, where we'd visit schools and be hosted by a local family during our second week of the program. After our general welcome in Tokyo, we formed into small groups and met our American colleagues, who we would travel with across the country. And every prefecture was assigned a special agent who would, in a sense, protect us. Ours was an old-school former member of the selected service guards. From what we could ascertain, he'd be assigned to international dignitaries as a bodyguard during state visits. Physically he was, upon first glance, an unassuming presence but I noticed that he always positioned himself in a place where he could watch all entrances and exits. His countenance was comforting.

What we Americans quickly learned about our hosts was how important ritual was in everyday life. Prior to our departure from JFK airport we all were given a list of potential faux pas Westerners frequently make when visiting Japan. There exists a code of properness in many of the small informalities that we would simply not consider or notice. For example, the handing out of business cards requires a certain protocol. To simply reach into one's wallet, pull out a business card, and hand it to whomever one is talking to is considered disrespectful.

Both the presenter and the receiver have certain obligations. In a manner of speaking, my business card and the way I present it reflect who I am and indirectly what sort of family I come from. If

I am haphazard in the presentation it suggests that I care very little about myself and even less about the person I am presenting the card to. To make the proper presentation, one holds the business card in cupped hands extended out toward the receiver and accompanies the presentation with a respectful bow. The receiver then takes the card, reads it very carefully, and in turn does the same. I found that if I were ever in doubt under any circumstance in my stay, I would throw in a few extra bows. One could never over-bow.

Following a week of visits to schools and meetings with our Japanese counterparts, we left our small groups and traveled with our hosts to their homes. Mr. and Mrs. Shimoyama were my hosts. They spoke very little English and I spoke very little Japanese, so most of our communication was done through pantomime and laughter. As is the custom, I brought gifts from my home state to formally present to them: two beautiful picture books of the southern Utah landscape and a Texas fifth of Johnny Walker Black Label. They loved the lunar landscape of the West but confessed, with a great deal of embarrassment, that neither one of them drank spirits. It occurred to me that perhaps the selection board, seeing that I resided in Utah, might have presumed I was a Mormon and paired me up with a Japanese couple that happened to be practicing members of the LDS faith. When I finally managed to communicate this idea, they both began laughing. They simply did not drink.

In return, the Shimoyamas gave me a beautiful spinning rod, an exquisitely ornate fan for my wife, a handmade pen of local hardwood for my daughter, and a samurai practice sword for my son. Each offering reflected something very specific that I'd written about my family in my personal narrative for the selection committee. The Shimoyamas knew considerably more about me than I knew about them.

Under "food interests" I'd written that I loved seafood and sushi, and for my first evening the Shimoyamas served a dinner specifically catered toward me. A variety of sushi had been carefully prepared and then, halfway through dinner, a local fisherman arrived at the house with a deep-ocean Japanese spider crab, prepared perfectly and spread out exquisitely on a large platter. I'd never seen anything like a spider crab in my life. The span of the legs when extended was easily three feet. I later discovered how difficult these particular crabs were to come by, and that they were the first my hosts had ever seen.

On the third day of my stay the Shimoyamas suggested we go for a drive through the countryside. That morning when I appeared from my room wearing a fly-fishing shirt with a Waterworks monogram on it as well as a hat with the same insignia, they smiled. Since we did a great deal of smiling and nodding with each other anyway, I thought very little of it.

Driving along the motorway, a truck passed our car and cut back into the passing lane a little too closely for Mr. Shimoyama. To my and Mrs. Shimoyama's surprise, he let loose with what I could only suspect were a host of profanities. I started laughing. It was so completely out of character for Mr. Shimoyama, and he apologized profusely for this sudden outburst. I told him not to worry— I was an expert at that sort of language. Very clearly he said, "Tell me what you say."

During the next half hour I gave them both lessons on the proper lexicon of road rage. Every time a car passed I'd say, "Go!" and they'd be off to the races. Try as they might, they couldn't sound angry.

We soon happened upon suspicious-looking fly-fishing water, and I was pleased when they eased the car off the road and down toward the river. Mr. Shimoyama spoke the name of the river to me in Japanese and then in English: "This is Sweet Fish River." Upstream, lining both sides of the riverbank, were men using what looked like spey rods. Mr. Shimoyama said, "Tenkara." He looked at me for approval, and I repeated back to him, "Tenkara." For a while we just stood looking at the water, then he suggested we roll up our pants and walk down by the fishermen. I realized my hosts had driven me to the water because my information sheet listed that I loved fly-fishing. It touched me deeply.

I pantomimed to Mr. Shimoyama, asking why there were no reels attached to these long rods. Again he nodded and said, "Tenkara," and I returned the same word to him. He motioned for me to follow him until we came within respectable distance of a fisherman. When the man noticed us Mr. Shimoyama bowed and spoke to him and nodded toward me. Immediately the man smiled and pointed to my hat. "Waterworks. Ketchum, Idaho. Silver Creek," he said. His name was Mr. Sankita, and in those three very abrupt phrases he'd conveyed a wealth of information to me about himself: he was a fly fisherman familiar with a small reel manufacturer from Ketchum, Idaho, and he could identify one of the legendary meccas of trout water in the western United States. Through a series of gestures he offered me the opportunity to cast his rod. I shrugged my shoulders to demonstrate that I had no idea how to use the rod, adding an elaborate gesture that suggested I hoped he would fish some more and that I, in turn, would then try my hand. When I further gesticulated a comment on the lack of a reel by reeling up an imaginary line on a fly reel and raising my eyebrows into question marks, he nodded that he understood and said, "Tenkara."

It was my first exposure to the world of Tenkara, an ancient Japanese form of fly-fishing that means "from the heavens." It requires very little equipment other than a Tenkara rod, traditionally made from bamboo; a fly line; and some flies. The line is about eighteen- to twenty-feet in length and perhaps 3x at the tippet. The cast itself is made in the same fashion as a spey cast but without a snap *T*. It's the sort one would use in a downstream cast if using nymphs or soft hackle.

I made one decent cast, but being in the water on the other side of the world, with another fisherman and two utterly thoughtful hosts, made me homesick in a way I couldn't explain. I missed my family, felt the weight of an uncertain world, and wondered what storm might come from the events of 9/11. We American Fulbright Memorial Scholars had been embraced and comforted by our Japanese hosts in the kindest of ways. I felt the pulse of water against my calves and reflected on how many occasions rivers had saved my life when I least expected it. I found myself trying to hold back tears and then surrendered to the moment. It felt good to cry, and if my hosts or fellow fly fisherman noticed, they were kind enough to turn away and allow me to save face.

EL GATO
AND THE SHADOW
———

I have been here before. Several times I think. I'm sure of it. And I look forward to being here, a stone's throw from the ocean on a rugged coastline that does not invite the casual and careless guest. There are black flags along the beach warning swimmers of dangerous undertows and riptides, but these American tourists—bolstered by cheap two-for-one Happy Hour drinks and the Four O'Clock Booze Team—are capable of doing incredibly stupid things. The first day, a middle-aged man, well liquored-up and encouraged by his group of friends, makes a beeline straight toward the Sea of Cortez. "Last one in buys the next round!" he screams over his shoulder. A belly flop, the howl of his friends, and then a tumble of ass and limbs. His friends are silenced. His wife or girlfriend screams. His bathing suit is ripped off. We all see this man and then he is gone. Somewhere under. Somewhere in the deep. And he doesn't resurface. There is no lifeguard on this beach and it says so in plain view in three languages. There *is* a large board that shows what happens to people in riptides. It's very clear. I wonder what the man's last thought was? Did he have children? Did he, in his last breath, say he loved them?

EL GATO RECOGNIZES me when I see him after a long walk along the beach. He smiles and we shake hands. I ask him about his daughter and his family. "If I remember correctly, your daughter is seventeen?"

"Yes," he replies. It means something to him that I remember.

El Gato drives a golf cart on the hotel property and he is very proud of his work. He tells me that his daughter will graduate this spring and she wants to leave home to become an actress. El Gato is worried. It would mean sending her to live in Mexico City, and Mexico City, he tells me, is a dangerous place for young girls. He asks me what I think he should do. I tell him the only thing I really know about being a father is that he must help his daughter do what will make her happy. I suspect this was not what he wanted to hear.

"Would you do such a thing?"

"I have, Gato, and it is not easy."

"But it was a good thing?"

"I think so."

"You have come with your wife and your children?"

"My wife. My children have grown up and they are living their lives. They are happy and I am happy for them."

For a while we just stand side by side and absorb the sunset together. We both understand it perfectly.

Finally El Gato says, "The Shadow is still alive."

"You have seen him?"

"Yes. And if you will stay here and wait until dark you might see him go back to the cave. The tide is coming in now."

The Shadow is a man who lives on the beach and survives by the ocean. He is a phantom, a mythic figure, a warning to children who wander too far from the resort. The resorts would like to get rid of him but they can't. It is his beach too.

"Have you ever talked to him?" I ask.

"No," El Gato replies. "It is not safe."

"Why?"

"Because some people think he is *la serpiente*."

"Do you think that is a truth?"

El Gato thinks about this for a moment and then shrugs his shoulders. "I don't know."

"Maybe he is just a man who loves the ocean."

"Yes. Maybe that is possible."

"El Gato," I say, measuring my words carefully, "I understand the Shadow. I admire people like him. He is a noble man perhaps."

El Gato nods his head and then excuses himself. "Well, I must return to the registration desk. We have many guests coming in."

"Of course," I reply. "It is good to see you again."

In the next seven days I will look for the Shadow when I can. I will climb up to his first cave. He will not be there. It is a comfortable space and from the entrance he has a panoramic view of the Sea of Cortez. From this vantage point he can observe the great whales—the humpback, blue, and gray—as they migrate to their birthing waters further south. This is not a crazy man. One morning I will walk the beach early, carrying with me a large bag of tortillas and ground coffee. I will leave it at the front of the second cave, the cooking cave.

I will not see the Shadow on this trip and I cannot be certain he still lives in these caves. But in the end it makes no difference to me at all. A part of the Shadow lives in me. It resides in the deepest part of me. It is the part I understand clearly, and it is the part I have the most difficulty trying to explain.

When I return to the casita Alana is just getting up. She is standing in the kitchenette and has poured herself a glass of mango juice.

"This is weird, but somebody took our coffee and tortillas." She thinks for a moment and says, "Do you think one of the housekeepers might have—"

But I stop her before she can finish the sentence. "I took them to the Shadow's cave. This morning."

"Seriously?"

"Yes."

"Why would you do something like that?"

"Because it was necessary and we can buy some more."

She regards me for the longest time and finally says in a resigned voice, "You know, sometimes I just don't get you at all."

And I reply, "Yes, I do know that."

She shakes her head, pads over to the coffee pot, and pours us both a cup.

SHARK

The charter boat was arranged for us by a friend of the guy who offers his services to my brother-in-law, Steve, and his wife, who live a great part of the year in a luxurious home in Cabo, Mexico. Joaquin is indispensable to my brother-in-law. He knows people who know people, the sort of man one needs to know if there is ever a problem. Joaquin is a man who makes things happen. Arrangements had been made to meet Joaquin in the early light at the Cabo Marina, where he would introduce us to our captain for a day of deep-sea fishing off the Sea of Cortez and out into the open waters of the Pacific Ocean.

My brother-in-law, his partner, Todd, and I walked along the dock admiring all the luxury fifty- and sixty-foot-deep marlin fishing boats: powerful twin and turbo diesels with chrome and pearl-shined hulls; the finest combat saltwater fishing gear; tournament-rigged, multi-level steerage components, thrusters, and inboard and outboard motors; names like *Marlin Thrasher* and *Kingpin* painted on the aft beams. These boats were substantial; anyone would feel comfortable heading off to the high seas in such crafts. It was not hard to imagine Hemingway or Joan and Lee Wulff squinting out of the harbor off along the horizon, imagining what fish the day might bring. What beautiful, plumed black Marlin from the deep and mysterious underworld might take a swipe at a lure or live bait and in doing so end up plasticized and hanging on a wall in Ketchum or beyond? We did not feel quite that romantic when Joaquin stopped between two very expensive and tricked-out charter boats to present the captain and our boat, *The Lucky One*. It was a rude awakening. The twenty-eight-foot craft was more fiberglass patchwork than boat. The toilet was not working but the captain, Carlos, assured us it was working last week. His son, Cesar, was the first mate, and Cesar's son, Little Cesar, age thirteen, was—I suppose—the second mate. All in all it was a rough crew but we liked them immediately. Little Cesar was a handsome young boy. He displayed a wonderful exuberance, doing a man's work in a boy's body. He was caught in the world between child and adolescent—flexing his muscles and showing the greenhorns how much he knew about this manly world, then quickly drifting off into daydreams, just a young kid on the ocean with his father and grandfather.

After we passed the safety inspection and offered our licenses to the Coast Guard, we fueled the diesels and cast off. A short mooring at Cesar's #1 bait guy to purchase needlenose, and flying fish were touted as the bait for the day. Then out toward open water. Carlos plunked the fish into the bait box. "Good for the marlin and dorado," he said. "Maybe even the roosterfish." It wasn't an overwhelming vote of confidence. I looked at my partners and they sort of shrugged their shoulders. Truly, it didn't matter. If we caught a fish, we caught a fish, and if we didn't, well so be it. Shortly after cutting out into the Pacific, one of the reels started screaming. I took the fighting seat while the butt end of a stocky pole was shoved into my hands. It was big and heavy, and the experience felt foreign to me. Three monstrous tugs, and whatever it was snapped off the line. On the retrieve I noticed it was cut clean. Surgical. Something big. Something mysterious.

"Barracuda?" I asked.

"Shark," Cesar replied.

The day was hot and muggy and the fishing was nonexistent. Carlos and the crew placed us in their favorite runs to no avail. Finally, around one o'clock, Steve landed a small skipjack. It was thrown into the live-bait box. Not long after that, I caught a slightly larger skipjack and it was also thrown into the bait box. Todd was next in the rotation and took the fighting seat. Jokingly I told him it was his turn to catch something larger, something that couldn't be stuffed into the bait box, and within a half hour he had hooked and landed a three-foot mako shark. Before he had time to suggest we release it, the crew gaffed the shark and clubbed it to death. The killing of the shark reminded me of something from *The Flintstones*. Once they gaffed the shark, Carlos grabbed a club the size of a policeman's baton and cracked the shark's skull, then gave high fives all around. We popped a cold Corona to celebrate.

I returned back into the fighting chair and regarded the shark. It was not more than a foot from where I planted my feet. I slipped the fighting harness on and jammed the pole into its holder. "Cesar," I said, "I don't think the shark is dead."

"It is very dead," he replied with a slight edge to his voice.

"But its gills are moving."

Suddenly the mako began thrashing about the deck, snapping its teeth and looking to grab any of us. It was mayhem, with Carlos and Cesar screaming and swinging wildly at the mako. Finally they pronounced the shark *muerto*. Dead.

We started to see a surprising number of sharks in a place Carlos had never seen them before, and I said we'd like to try to catch another shark. The caveat was that I'd like to do it on a fly.

"That will not work," Cesar said, "because sharks like to chase the wounded fish. They go for the blood."

I finally convinced him to let me give it a try.

"But we do not have the fly," he said, hoping to put an end to the mad gringo's notion of what might catch a shark.

I slid out of the fighting chair, dropped into the cabin, and returned with a Big Red shark fly rigged with wire tippet I'd found on the floor of the cabin.

Before attaching the fly on, the Cesars baited both the port and starboard side with fresh fish. Almost reluctantly they attached the fly to my line. Pulling off about twenty feet of line, I let it slide out behind *The Lucky One.*

It could not have been more than five minutes before my pole jerked and I set the hook hard. Big Cesar and Little Cesar jumped into action and retrieved the other lines while my reel screamed. It was something big. Big. BIG.

About thirty feet out, cutting a tight line from port to starboard, we all saw it. The fin.

"SHARK!" Cesar yelled.

The water split open as a seven-foot mako shark cartwheeled into the air. Midair it shook the fly but instinct made me set hard, and the shark crashed into the sea. It clearly took me by surprise and unhinged me. I wasn't prepared for the violent slam against the fly, the lightning speed at which everything happened in an instant. Adrenalin coursed through me and my hands were shaking.

I began a slow retrieve when the line straightened and pulled against the drag. Somehow the shark was still on the line. I'd seen it throw the fly—we'd all seen it so this made no sense. Carlos threw the boat into reverse so I could get line on the reel but it was clearly taking more line than I could retrieve.

"This is a big shark," Cesar said. "What would you like to do?"

It hadn't occurred to me. I've kept only two fish in the last forty years—a striper and a bluefish—at the request of my hosts when I fly-fished off the coast of Martha's Vineyard.

"I don't know," I said and looked at my fishing mates. "What are your thoughts?"

"How many times in your life do you think you'll catch a shark on a fly?" Todd asked me.

"Probably never again."

"Then I think you should keep it. Plus, they're good eating."

"I'd like to keep it if I can land it, Cesar," I replied.

With the decision finalized, I set about attempting to land the shark. What I wish I could write is that I remembered every single moment of the fight but it would not be the truth. Certainly in the beginning I was nervous, unprepared for what lie ahead. But once I began to familiarize myself with the mechanics, the brutal physics of landing a shark, I settled down into a slow and methodical death dance. It took well over a half hour to reel the mako close enough to the stern that we could realize its size.

The mako's silhouette was a radiant mix between cyan and chartreuse, and shimmied brilliantly underneath the rolling waves. We all felt a certain reverence for its brute strength and beauty. Against the deep, dark blue of the ocean it appeared luminescent and unearthly. It was so exquisitely beautiful I would not have been surprised if it breached the surface and took flight.

A silence fell over the boat and the only sound was the muffled throated rumblings of the twin-diesel engines idling. I tried to gain some ground on the mako but for every ten feet I could get on the reel, it seemed to take fifteen back. Todd and Steve whispered encouragement and offered me water. Part of me wanted to cut the leader and let the mako disappear into the underworld but something decidedly larger was going on inside me. I was thinking about my ten-year battle with cancer, that dark and dangerous disease lurking somewhere under the surface of my skin. How with each clinical trial, every bout of radiation, every toxic injection, I'm losing ground and my strength diminishes. It's a predatory disease. An unemotional opportunist. A perfect killing machine.

It was not the mako shark I fought that afternoon. It was my own disease. The frightening unknown of it. The brutal and violent swiftness of it. The darkness under the surface. It was all there, being acted out in a brutal struggle. Life and death. Today it would not be me, but when my time came, I would be ready.

LAY ME DOWN

———

Death has been on my mind lately. There have been my own medical issues, of course, but that is not all of it. It is both larger and smaller than the scope of the inevitable. I have unexpectedly lost friends this year—great people who are supposed to be here but aren't—and this is bitter. It is difficult to accept.

I suspect it has a great deal to do with the lack of the steelhead season as well. If I am being completely truthful, I am more worried about the earth than I am about myself. When you are of a place and you carry it in your bones for a lifetime, you can see and feel even the subtlest changes.

I have been married to the landscape of Stanley, Idaho, and the Salmon River for thirty years. And every one of those years, as the months draw closer to April steelhead season, the chatter between the Captain and me picks up. We talk with each other early in the mornings because neither of us sleeps well until we are on the water—in the company of each other and our other steelhead brothers. We have performed this spring ritual for more years than I can easily remember. The talk centers on the essentials: temperature, the sudden fluctuations of river conditions, clarity of the water, forecasts for the coming week, snow conditions, human traffic on the water, and—most important—the steelhead counts from the Sawtooth Fish Hatchery.

The Captain lives for steelhead fishing and during the year works hundreds of hours of overtime so he can take the entire month of April to do what he most loves to do: fly-fish for steelhead. We have access to the Carstensens' ranch on Crooked Creek and, if we are fortunate, they join us and we fly-fish, eat well, and drink healthily together during much of that time. It is a lifeline away from the outside world, and it eases the effects, at least momentarily, of the toxins. We meet together to fish because it takes us deeper.

I am fortunate because my wife has always understood the importance of this ritual. As I prepare to leave, I often feel like a young schoolboy completely packed and ready for his first summer camping trip, and she teases me about my excitement.

Early reports of an anomaly in the weather have the Captain greatly concerned. The Stanley Basin, particularly the upper reach of river we fish, has been seeing unusually warm weather. The climate in the past ten years has changed noticeably, and it's foolish to deny the science of global warming. The body of evidence is too indisputable. The Salmon River has become more unpredictable each year, which presents its own set of dangers. Familiar runs can become unfamiliar, and that can be deadly and vicious.

If the temperature rises too quickly and it doesn't freeze at night, the canyon dumps tons of mud and silt into the Salmon River, making it impossible to see beneath the surface of the water. The river becomes, at first, tea-colored, then finally coffee-brown. Because our style of fly-fishing requires that we must be able to see the steelhead, to spot them, a runoff of this sort will be the end of the season. Even under the best of conditions, in the best years, the weather is always a gamble. Steelhead are difficult to spot. Their silver bodies so beautifully camouflaged against the silvered glint of the river's underbelly that it takes a trained eye to unlock the water. The Captain has such an eye, and has taught us all how to read the water.

After the Captain gets settled into the cabin, cuts a path through the snow and ice, stacks firewood for the month, and makes it comfortable for us, he stalks the river, hunting for steelhead. In the evening he calls me to report on his findings, and I hang on to the words as if they were spoken in some coded, sacred language of fish. To an outsider it would sound like pure gibberish, but I can see exactly the spot and hold of water.

"Nothing at the Fish Factory yet; the Death Wade is still too shallow, and the water is thin at the dump" not only informs me of the water level, identifies an exact location, offers me an idea of the steelhead count, and gives me clinical observations of the river, but also it paints a complete narrative of what I can expect.

This year, when the Captain calls, there is a gravitas in his voice that I have not heard before. It is tangible, and I am hoping that I have misunderstood what I have come to sense is inevitable: the Salmon River has blown out. Finally, less than a week before I depart, I know I am on the far side of hope.

The snow pack is melting rapidly, and the Salmon is rising daily. To not heed these warnings would be foolish. And the difference between surviving an accident and being the victim of one can be a simple misstep in the rush and pulse of water. In the spring, when it can be fifteen below zero, every single mistake is compounded by the cold.

"The water is running high and fast, and you know how dangerous that can be," the Captain says.

I certainly did, and I instantly had a flashback to a moment many summers ago when I was running the Stanley writing workshop and almost drowned on the Salmon River. I still get a chill thinking about it. Midweek of the first week, we would take our students on a half-day river trip, beginning at Mormon Bend and taking out below Sunbeam Dam. For several years, Ron Gillett, owner of Triangle C Rafting, would offer us an early-season discount, and use the trip as a tune-up for his own returning river rats and the new crew. Gillett was a good boss and had a solid reputation for running a tight and safe operation.

We divided the students up into rafts, keeping a balance of returning river rats, new crew, and students who had absolutely no experience at all in the wilderness. Mormon Bend was a perfect place to launch the rafts because there was plenty of time to smooth out kinks with guests before moving into the rapids. I'd worked as a river guide in southern Utah before, and this summer Ron asked if I wouldn't mind making a run with one of his new guides.

"Just to kind of see how he does…how he is with guests," offered Ron.

No sooner had we launched than the weather started to sour. The students were well-insulated with wetsuits, life jackets, and layers of clothes. They'd stay warm because everybody contributed to paddling and had become—almost instantly—a member of the crew. Mine was the last raft, hanging back to pick up anybody who might go overboard during the run. Plowing through the rapids, the students could be heard screaming and flexing their newfound river muscle. There is something so wonderfully primal and empowering about being on the river, thinking that, to some degree, it can be tamed and you are part of this complex equation.

In a stretch of river called Piece of Cake our raft got a horrific gust of wind that virtually lifted the nose out of the water, putting us at a dangerous angle for approaching a series of rapids. The guide barked out a series of quick commands, exactly the same as I would have done under the same circumstances, but it was too late. In a split second, the raft flipped and we were all ejected into the icy water. I was sucked into a whirlpool and washing-machined over and over again. I wasn't able to get to the surface. The force of the water ripped my tennis shoes from my feet and pulled my shorts down around my ankles. I was in deep trouble and knew it.

The safety tips clients get before even getting on the river are standard practice for all outfitters. I could hear my own voice: *Remember, if you get thrown and pulled under the water, try and relax. Don't fight the water and it will spit you out. Don't panic!*

In the fray of it all, in the tumultuous bashing against rock and the ensuing disorientation, it is almost impossible to obey these commands. There is such a natural compulsion to fight the violence with struggle that it seems counterintuitive to relax. I wasn't able to practice my own advice, and at the moment when I knew I could not hold my breath any longer, I actually laughed. I thought of my wife and children, and of the irony that this was one of the few raft trips where I was actually a guest and here I was about to drown at my own game. I exhaled and surrendered myself to the turbulence, and was instantly spit up and out of water long enough to snatch a gasp of air before being pulled back down into the bosom of the Salmon.

Suddenly the Captain's voice on the telephone brought me back: "A couple of us are going to go out tomorrow and see if there is any place on the river we can spot steelhead. It isn't likely, but it's worth a try. I'll give you a call in the next day or so."

Until then, I'd be left to mope in my own selfishness.

TWO DAYS LATER, the Captain called. The verdict hung in his voice, and I knew how extremely difficult it was for him to admit it: the season had blown out. "I'm sorry, it's not going to happen this year."

"Goddamnit," I cursed. "Son of a bitch!"

"I'm sorry, Metcalf," he said, as though this had anything to do with him.

"I know it's selfish, but I'm just going to miss you and the boys."

"Me too." There was something else on his mind. He cleared his throat before talking. "You remember Jane's son, Mark?"

"Of course," I said, sort of annoyed he'd asked me. He knew that I knew him. Jane McCoy ran McCoy's Tackle Shop in Stanley, and I'd known her and her family for over twenty years. Mark was an accomplished musician who played for Micky and the Motorcars, and split his time between Stanley and Austin, Texas. He was also a terrific fly-fishing guide who had grown up on the river and knew it intimately. During steelhead season, he'd come back home to help his mother open up the shop and guide when he could.

"He drowned." I could hear the Captain choking back tears.

"What happened?" I was stupefied.

"He and a buddy wanted to go steelhead fishing but the river was too high and dangerous. They decided to take a raft and float the backside of Mormon Bend."

"So what happened exactly?"

"They put in and began fishing. Coming around Mormon Bend they hit a submerged tree that slit the tubes and both men got thrown into the river. The one guy managed to swim to shore but they haven't found Mark's body."

"Jesus Christ! At Mormon Bend? When did it happen?"

"The twenty-first. They've been searching for his body. No luck."

"How's Jane doing?"

"She's a wreck. A complete wreck." The Captain paused, trying to collect himself. "The whole town is broke up pretty bad."

"I'm so sorry to hear this. I don't know how you could ever survive something like that."

"They're probably going to call off the search in a day or so, and that will just kill Jane. She's been walking the river looking for Mark's body. You wouldn't even recognize her."

"That's so fucked up."

"Worse than that, Mark's girlfriend is the head of Search and Rescue."

The Captain's kids had grown up with Mark; it gets personal pretty quickly in small towns. The other man who survived worked for the Captain on his road crew for three and a half years.

When Search and Rescue called off the search, Mark's girlfriend and Jane continued on their own. A few days later, two steelhead fishermen found Mark's body in the back eddy below Sunbeam Dam.

Mark's girlfriend told a friend of ours that the best part of every day was waking up in the morning and having Mark's head lying on her shoulder. And when she came upon his body, this is exactly how she lifted him from the river.

THE UNSPOKEN

*All rivers race to the heat of the heart, where water whispers a
name and a place, spreads itself flat, stops waving goodbye and
returns to reflect the green shore.*

—Roslyn Nelson

For more than two decades I have marked my life by the April steelhead run on the Salmon River, in the broad embrace of the Sawtooth
Mountains' jagged granite teeth.

I have marked these years in equal measure of friendship,
laughter, the escape from civilization, and the knowledge that I
am—if only briefly—a guest in this ritual life dance of a dying species: the great oceangoing rainbow trout, the steelhead. Illusionists
of light and shadow, these anadromous steelhead travel over nine
hundred miles to spawn in their original redds on the Salmon. The
biological need to reproduce. Such instinct for survival. The possibility of life. A beautiful thing, life.

For the past two days, temperatures outside the hand-hewn
log cabin on Crooked Creek Ranch have not been above zero. This
year, spring has refused to arrive and holds stubborn to the particulars of the land. A fire crackles in our cast-iron stove and the cabin
breathes and groans with its own winter songs. Stiff, dark coffee per-
colates in a battered pot, the aromatic smell of dark Arabian beans
as seductive and mysterious as life itself.

I have come a few days before the others so the Captain and I
can fish together before the rest of the gang arrives to join us. We
begin a slow and ritualistic chorus in preparation for the morning.

The conversation is stripped of anything but the essentials. In all honesty, we have said it all before. Our morning chatter is liturgical and measured in ritual.

"It's going to be a cold one."

"Yes, it is."

"I hope we can see them today."

"It'll be difficult."

"Yes, it will."

And it will. These are true words. There is no room for anything else in this landscape of snow, ice, the gurgling of the river, and steelhead. This is a small part of the beauty. There is a reason I have arrived early this season to steelhead fish with the Captain. I need to talk with him about my health. But in two days, I have said nothing.

To put these words into the universe makes me feel as though I will begin to disappear. My health issues are real enough. I am not a foolish man. There are medical facts and mathematical percentages and still I can't help but feel that this water contains medicine and magic in equal weight. In the rumble of water over rock, the Salmon River whispers to me of its own sacred medicine. So I say nothing.

The serpentine road downriver from lower Stanley is slick with a layer of snow-covered ice. We pay attention. Around the bend, a smashed sports car reminds us there are no second chances. Frozen rocks, loosened by the breathing of the canyon walls, have crashed onto the slender two-lane highway. A herd of elk, dusted in snow, huddles close to the road. A giant bull stands guard over the herd, measuring the threat of danger. And when our rig gets close enough to see into his deep, mercurial eyes, he is done with us. We are not a threat and he turns away, toward the sweeping basin, to watch for wolves. It has been a harsh, brutal winter in the Stanley Basin. The herd looks thin and weary, and I say so.

Sixteen years ago, over a dozen wolves were released in central Idaho by the state's wildlife agency, protected through the

Endangered Species Act. Immediately, lines were drawn between conservationists, local farmers, and sheepherders. At the center of this maelstrom, fervently against the reintroduction of wolves into the wilds, was Ron Gillett. The rugged landscape of the Salmon River and the great Stanley Basin have provided him with a good living.

"Did you hear what happened with Ron and the Wolf Lady?" the Captain asks.

"No," I reply, thankful for the distraction.

"You know how he hates the wolves?"

"Yes," I say, pouring us both a cup of coffee from a battered Stanley thermos.

"Well, he's driving into town, when he sees the Wolf Lady taking photographs of wolves frolicking in the snow. Ron pulls his rig over, jumps out with his .22 rifle, and starts yelling at her."

"You've got to be kidding?"

"So the Wolf Lady turns her camera on Ron and starts shooting off pictures."

"And?"

"They got into some sort of scuffle. The Wolf Lady claimed Ron tried to grab the camera from her. She ended up falling to the ground. They've been at it for some time."

"What's the punch line?"

"Ron got thrown in the tank overnight. There'll be a trial in July or August."

"What do you think will happen?"

The Captain blew on his coffee, took a sip, and chuckled.

"Stupid question." The Captain nods his head. We both know the outcome.

Four months later, Ron walked out of a Custer County courtroom a free man. It was justice in northern Idaho. Nobody was surprised.

Winter months in this landscape can break even the hardiest of people. Stories are told and retold of townspeople who got "cabin fever" and just "up and left," people who disappeared or committed suicide or drank themselves to death. It's rare, but it happens.

As an outsider these narratives beg questions: How and why does this happen? What is the pathology of this winter landscape? How do things fester in us? Is it one thing that becomes another and we finally snap?

There is a poison in Ron that does not fit how he has governed himself on the river. At the mention of healthy wolf packs he can hardly control himself. One of his frequent battle cries in preaching the anti-wolf gospel is: "We don't care if you nuke 'em or poison 'em, just as long as they're gone!" If possible, he would rid the West of all wolves. This frenzied madness plays well in this landscape of ranchers and sheepherders but it is hollow and vacuous. For Ron, it is consumptive and leaves little room for reflection and balance.

"It's like a cancer and it's eating Ron up, them wolves."

There it was, the opening I needed to talk to the Captain about the aggressive return of my own cancer. I'd promised my wife I would speak to the boys, to keep it all out front and on the table. I'd practiced what I would say and knew it would not be an easy conversation for either of us.

In the most profound and sacred ways, the Captain and I are brothers. We go deeper with each other than we do with our own kin. Still, we tend to keep our emotional cards close to the table. I am good at this, but the Captain is much better. I began slowly, trying to get the words right in my mind.

"Speaking of cancer ..." I said, clearing my throat.

The Captain interrupted me. "Pull over. A pair of steelhead."

I eased my rig off onto the shoulder of the road. The Captain was out onto the pavement headhunting for steelhead before I could yank on the emergency brake.

"A male and a female."

"Where?"

"See the dead branch, directly across the river?"

"Just above the white pyramid rock?"

"Yes."

My eyes strained. I hadn't been back on the river long enough to shift to my steelhead eyes.

"Can you see them?" the Captain asked.

"How far out from the pyramid rock?"

"On our side, up about a rod length."

Again, I tried to focus. First I looked upstream, distracting myself by the canyon walls with the hope that I might then be able to see what the Captain often calls "the absence of what should be there." He didn't press me.

Seconds before I was about to confess I'd failed, the female fanned over the redd. Moments later, a large male slid over and held to her side. We moved slowly, staying low and in the shadows, hardly breathing. Every so often the Captain stopped in his tracks and studied the river.

"Grab your rod and go cast to the male. I'll spot."

"That's not going to happen," I replied stubbornly.

"I've been up here a week, Metcalf. Go get your rod."

"Rock, paper, scissors," I suggested, pounding my fist into an open palm.

It's not that either one of us wouldn't die to be the first to cast to this large rogue male, but the Captain's generosity is such that he will not fish until his friends have all cast. I threw down paper to the Captain's rock. I assembled my 8-weight rod. The Captain selected a couple of flies and we talked about the best way to approach the male.

"We'll both cross the Death Wade. Drop below the male and work upriver. I'll cross above and spot for you." As we slid into the Salmon I began to tense up. The Captain offered calm words. "Take your time. No rush."

This stretch of water is always dangerous, and I am not fond of it. I pushed against the current and my footing was uncertain. A slip here would be disastrous.

After working my way through the tongue, I paused and tried to settle down. The Captain was climbing up a scramble of rock, already on the other side.

For a moment I closed my eyes. The sounds of the Salmon began to soothe and calm me. It was a transformation so absolute and complete that I knew the conversation I'd planned to have with the Captain about my own health issues would likely not happen. I'd come home again. When I opened my eyes and looked to the Captain, he quickly signaled me with his hands.

Hold up. The male is moving.

The Captain gestured to the water. The light from my vantage point was poor. In the general vicinity where the Captain had pointed, the river suddenly erupted in a violent swirl of fins and tails. A small male had probably tried to slide alongside the spawning female.

"He'll be back," the Captain yelled to me, "as long as she stays put or until he gets his ass kicked good. Let them settle down before casting."

I stood in the river, waiting. Sunlight began to appear and slowly cut a diagonal slash of light against the canyon wall. The river glimmered in deep-flecked grays and oranges, reflections from the tumble of river rock. The chorus of the Salmon became, at once, hypnotic and soothing.

"Ready to cast?"

"Yes."

"Can you see them?"

I nodded.

"Okay. Cast about three feet above them, almost against the bank, and let the fly swing directly in front of them."

I pulled line off my 8-weight and let it float behind me until I'd reeled off what I thought I'd need for a proper cast. I made several false casts directly upriver until the line was measured and then I shot the line diagonally above the holding steelhead. It was a perfect cast, the weighted fly sliding directly in front of the male.

"Good to see you haven't forgotten how to cast," the Captain yelled over the water, adding—as he often does—"Same thing. Same place."

Again, I made the same cast. And again. And again. The pair held tight.

"Tie on something different."

"Something dark?"

"Your guess is as good as mine."

I withdrew a fly box from my vest, studied the collection of brightly colored steelhead patterns, and selected a Halloween fly. I tied it on to my tippet and crimped the hook. I submerged the tip of my fly rod into the river to break up the ice that had formed on the guides.

Again, I began false casting. When distance was stretched out, I shot the line exactly where I had placed several dozen unsuccessful casts. This time was different. The instant the fly passed close to the female, the male struck violently, the water exploding into silver crystals, and the run was on.

Instinctively, the steelhead torpedoed toward a cluster of giant angular granite boulders directly upriver, trying to sever the fly line. If I couldn't properly work this fish soon, it would all be over. Line screamed through the reel. I tightened the drag.

"Can you turn him?" the Captain yelled.

"I don't know!"

The brutal raw strength of the steelhead was stunning. It exploded through the surface of the water into a cartwheel and slowed for just a second.

"If he gets wrapped around those rocks, he'll bust you off."

I knew that. I was getting dangerously close to the backing on my reel. I leaned hard on my fly rod and tightened the drag to a dangerous point, but the steelhead wasn't tiring. My arms were starting to feel the burn. For a split second, the steelhead seemed unable to make any headway, and under the impression I had some control over this moment, I relaxed. The steelhead reversed directions and beelined directly toward me. Madly, I stripped line as rapidly as I could. In an instant he jetted by me and made an abrupt cut to the tongue of the river, where the current could be worked against me.

"Jesus! Did you see the size of him?" I yelled.

"You've got to chase him downriver or you'll lose him! See if you can work him to the bank. I'll head downriver and see you in Challis," he cackled before making his way to the bank, grabbing his large steelhead net, and hustling downriver. Then he hollered something from the bank. Although I couldn't hear him, I had some sense of his advice: "Keep your rod tip up!"

I knew the steelhead was getting the better of me. I took off downriver, trying to keep my feet spread apart and balanced. Stumbling at this point would be catastrophic.

Quickly enough I was in the seam of the fast water, exactly where I didn't want to be. I was moving into treacherous territory, and I'd lost sight of the Captain. In a way, I was relieved, because he would be chiding me about going for a "swim" if I didn't turn the steelhead soon.

A sudden shift in footing and I stumbled into the river. I struggled to keep upright. I was bent almost to the knee; water topped the bib line of my waders and a slosh of freezing water streamed into my boots. It could have been worse. I could have gone under.

Somehow in the chaos, I managed to keep the rod tip upright and the steelhead on. Slowly I regained my composure and settled down to matters at hand. The Captain was a speck downriver, descending a steep shale slope to where he believed I'd be able to land the fish. I had some good fortune—the steelhead swung in a huge arch from the deep water and moved into a stretch of current I could handle.

My fly line grew taut and hummed its own particular music as the steelhead cut downriver toward the proper side of the bank. Then, surprisingly, he began a slow, determined course upriver toward the female's redd. This shift gave me valuable time to gain slack line back on to my reel.

When the steelhead was parallel to me, I got my first good, close look at him. He was magnificent, with thick shoulders; a deep steel-blue cast along his back and head; and a wide, rich crimson-almost-burgundy stripe along his side. I could clearly see the fly sunk deep into his jaw.

There was a slight slack in the line and I was cautious not to reel it taut until I could move closer to the bank and gain better footing. A slight twist in my footing rumbled rocks, and the male shuddered. I braced for what I expected to be a run. Instead, the steelhead pulled parallel to the female and held. He was spent. In what must have felt like his final moments in the Salmon River, this steelhead refused a last run and, in turn, followed the deep biological instinct to complete a life cycle.

Slowly, I was able to get to the bank, firm up my footing, and land the steelhead. He was massive—talon scarred across his back, a chunk chomped from his tail, firm and spent. I took him back to the water, held his tail, held my thumb on his lower jaw, and moved him slowly back and forth in the current, talking to him, offering thanks before releasing him into the safety of the Salmon.

I sat on the bank and looked downriver as the Captain waved his approval. I closed my eyes and savored this moment with deep appreciation and respect. In this instant, my world was as close to being perfect as I could hope.

I thought of my early-morning awkwardness in trying to talk to the Captain about my health. In truth, what did I really need to tell my best friend? Would I say that my surgery, radiation, and hormonal treatment had not been successful? Did I need to tell him that in all probability we would not get as much time to fish together as either of us would like? I suspect in his own way, the Captain already knew these things.

When he joined me at the bank of the river, I told him the only truth I really knew: "That, my friend, was a noble steelhead."

"Yes, it was," he replied. He dug inside his steelhead jacket, pulled out a pack of Marlboro Lights, and offered me one. After a few moments of silence, he said, "It's good to see you again."

All I could say in reply was, "And the same back to you." It was all that was necessary.

ACKNOWLEDGMENTS

John Alley (University of Utah Press) for his keen editorial eye; Taft-Nicholson Artist-in-Residency program for granting me time in a sacred landscape to work; Terry and Hans Carstensen for offering me space at Crooked Creek; Tim Bywater for his thoughtful comments on the manuscript; and James Barilla for his careful review of the manuscript.

Special thanks to Dave Hall, who designed the cover for this collection, and Nikki Bazar for sharp editing of the text.

To the men and women of FFF and steelheading: Bill Selvage, Maggie Selvage, Steve Cole, John Wells, Karl Neubauer, and Eric Adams.

The Cox family for Bermuda and Alaska.

The regulars: Max Werner, JD Davis, Patrick Tovatt, Kelli Parker, Jay Bundy, David Kranes, Gene Jensen, Nicholas Calabro, BT, Todd Smith, and Mark Bergstrom.

My Croatian brothers: Petar Bijuk, Vjekoslav Vrbanic, and Josip Librenjak.

The following essays were previously published:

"The Last Steelhead" in *Western Humanities Review*; *Drake Magazine*; and *Requiem for the Living: A Memoir* (Salt Lake City, University of Utah Press, 2014).

"Unspoken," "Three Down," and "Lay Me Down" in *Requiem for the Living: A Memoir*.